The Red and Blacks of 1909 would experience another losing season, going 1-4-2 on the year. But this would be their last losing season until 1914.

The University of Georgia Red and Blacks 1909 Football team.
Robert Cooper Davis is second from the right in the third row.

"They're not that different from you, are they? (Pointing to a picture in an old school annual.) Same haircuts. Full of hormones, just like you. Invincible, just like you feel. The world is their oyster. They believe they're destined for great things, just like many of you. Their eyes are full of hope, just like you. Did they wait until it was too late to make from their lives even one iota of what they were capable? Because you see, gentlemen, these boys are now fertilizing daffodils. But if you listen real close, you can hear them whisper their legacy to you. Go on, lean in. Listen. You hear it?... Carpe... Hear it?... Carpe. Carpe diem.
Seize the day, boys. Make your lives extraordinary."
-Robin Williams as John Keating in
The Dead Poets Society

&MCG

February 15, 1977

Mr. John C. McHugh
P.O. Box 7343
Dahlonega, Georgia 30533

Dear Mr. McHugh:

The Admissions Committee of the School of Medicine at the Medical
College of Georgia is pleased to offer you a place in the September
1977 Class.

Your attention is called to the enclosed Information and Instruction
Sheet. The Admissions Committee reserves the right to withdraw your
acceptance if you fail to comply with the requirements as stated
thereon.

Your selection was made from a group of very outstanding applicants
The Committee feels that you are an excellent prospective physician
and all of us here at the Medical College of Georgia are happy that
you will be joining our student body.

Sincerely,

James B. Puryear, Ph.D.
Director of Student Affairs

JBP:ss

Enclosures (3)

Congratulations

Rick Litz

&MCG

CERTIFIED

141001

109
JOHN CLAY McH
PO BOX 7343
DAHLONEGA

The Goal.

To the Graduate:

You're a weed...but a weed with potential.

John McHugh M.D.

To the Graduate: You're a Weed...but a Weed with Potential.
John McHugh M.D.
Copyright © 2018 by Jennie Cooper Press
Pictures are in the public domain or property of the author except for photo of Steve
Jobs by Matthew Yohe, Socrates by Eric Gaba and Maya Agelou by Adria Richards.
Special thanks to Nancy Martz
All rights reserved. ISBN-13: 978-0988661868
Email: jc_mchugh@yahoo.com

Jennie Cooper Press
"Calm as a Hurricane"

*What is a weed? A plant whose virtues have
not yet been discovered.
-Ralph Waldo Emerson*

For Jennie Cooper, Bessie Clay, Rushton and Karen.

Table of Contents

-Dr. W.

-My Damn Eyes

-Janice Watts

-Karen

The three A's of success...Availability, Affability, and Ability...and in that order of importance.
-William Osler

Preface

I have always been bad about saving things. When I was in high school, I had a Juicy Fruit box in which I kept anything I thought was important or had a memory associated with it. The items are primarily from high school and college. After college I did the same thing, except then I put everything in a filing cabinet. Much to my wife's chagrin, I have every letter and post card she ever sent me. After forty-five years of lugging the box around with each move, I recently decided to look through it. In many ways, the letters, pictures, and other memorabilia evoked emotion and sadness. The past, of course, is always better as you remember it than it actually was. At the very bottom of the box was the original draft of a speech I gave at my high school graduation commencement. As I remember it, the senior class voted on four students to speak and then the teacher advisor, after hearing the speeches, determined the order in which they would be given. Let me be clear, the fact that I was among those chosen was not because of my grades. I barely had a ninety average and I had to bargain with an English teacher to let me do extra credit work to change an eighty nine average to ninety. Mine was chosen to be last. When I gave my speech to the teacher, I purposely left out the last line, "I was damn proud to be a Granger!" I could not wait to give the speech at the commencement and use the word "damn" as the last thing I'd say in high school in front of the students, teachers, and best of all, my mother. My mother was a LaGrange High Granger alum, Class of 1938, and everything she was a part of she loved whether it was being a Granger, being in the Coast Guard, or going back to college at age fifty-five.

As I was reading the speech that I had written at age eighteen in 1973, I was taken by the maturity of what I said. The whole speech was about encouraging my classmates to embrace their future, taking advantage of both the high school education and of all the people who had helped them get to this point. Although I did not know what a self-help book was or had I ever read one, the speech was a series of self-help concepts. Then it dawned on me where everything in the speech came from...my mother. As you'll see, the things I wrote do not match the expected mindset of an eighteen year old. I adored my mother and when she told me things, I listened. She had a saying for every situation and tended to respond with an aphorism rather than debate an issue. For instance, if I said I was going to do something she felt was unwise and she advised against it, but I planned to do it anyway, I'd get from her, "Suit yourself" or "To each his own." The tone of voice which she used to embellish the saying spoke volumes. If she did something you did not understand she would simply say, "I have a method in my madness." The one she'd say the most and the one I feel is probably the most powerful self-help tip she gave me, and in many ways responsible for my success is, "John, do not choose short term gratification over long term gain." This has resonated with me indelibly throughout my career.

The realization that the speech was a mini self-help book of sorts is how I got the idea for this project. I took each concept from the speech and associated it with quotes of historical and successful people. Many of the famous self-help authors have used the concepts my mother imparted to me. Then there is a sentence from the speech that states, "You have the task of fulfilling the dreams of those who love you." To me this is a huge and often overlooked responsibility of youth. Too often they only see themselves and too often all of us think we are in a vacuum, whether it be in success or failure. It is healthy to take credit for your failures but it is not healthy to take all the credit for your successes. There are people who love you who have been there for you and often times behind the scene. Yes, I feel you owe something to the people who love you. You owe it to them to be the very best you can be and to achieve what you are capable of. Having this concept in mind, I began to think of people who had helped me along the way. Well the list goes on and on and here's the dirty little secret, I thought I got into college, got into medical school, finished my urology residency, practiced medicine, and became a multimillionaire all on my own. This is far from the truth. I have listed several special people who have been important to me and my success. The sad thing is that some of them, although I remember them well, I hadn't really given them the credit they deserved for being there at a particular time of my life.

My hope is that some of the concepts of the speech and the illustrative quotes will spark some encouragement for the graduate. I also hope that my story told through the people who have helped me will prompt the reader to both acknowledge those important to you and to instill in you the concept of your responsibility to "make your parents proud." In doing so, you will have fulfilled their dreams for you and as a result, you will have fulfilled your potential. After all, fulfilling your full potential is what the people who love you want for you.

We are all weeds.....
Emerson said that a weed is a plant whose virtues have not yet been discovered. What we do now dictates whether we will be a weed the rest of our life. Who wants to weed. Something that is not wanted by society and often discarded. The decision is yours because the direction in which you point your education will determine your future.

Set goals that reach a little further than your talents dictate, and pursue them. In that way you will realize your goals and in turn you will have bettered yourself. Everyone must better himself. One is naive to rationalize that one can wait for developments because there is not that much time. Time waits for no man and is not going to start and you are no exception so act now. Decide. Decide what you want to do - align your decisions with your capabilities and pursue it. Put together all that school has given you.

Y ou'll notice in the speech there are numerous errors in spelling and in grammar, neither of which has ever been a strong suit of mine. Despite this, I minored in English literature in college and loved it. There might be a message in this that will apply to you. Can't spell? It doesn't mean you can't write a book.

When I gave this speech, I did not use notes. I had rehearsed it umpteen times and felt the delivery would be more impassioned without having to look down to read. Unfortunately, I forgot everything after saying, "We are all weeds." After a lengthy and uncomfortable pause I said, "Excuse me. I am going to start over." From that point on the speech luckily came back to me and I delivered it well. Years later my brother Jeff, who was in sixth grade at the time and in the audience said, "John that is the sorriest I have ever felt for you. You just stood there for what seemed like forever before you started talking again." If at first you don't succeed, try, try again!

The Speech

We are all weeds....

Emerson said that a weed is a plant whose virtues have not yet been discovered. What we do now dictates whether we will be a weed the rest of our life. Who wants to be a weed? Something that is not wanted and often discarded; a weed of society. He takes; he never gives. The decision is yours because the direction in which you point your education will determine your future.

Assign goals that reach a little further than your talents dictate, and pursue them. In this way, you will realize your goals and in turn you will have bettered yourself. Everyone must better himself. One is naïve to rationalize that one can wait for developments because there is not that much time. Time waits for no man and you are no exception so act now. Decide. Decide what you want to do. Align your decisions with your capabilities and pursue it. Put together all that school has given you and make it work.

Block out apathy and its constituents and counter with a concern for yourself. The pressure is on. You have the task of fulfilling the dreams of those who love you. That means a lot, the ones who love you, because they are the ones who got you here and it is their effect on your past which will determine your future. Think about that. A lot of hope has been placed on your education. They realize the long-term gain involved.

Let's take for instance the simple art of communication. What if we could not communicate with our peers in matters of importance ranging from gossip to politics? Clark Gable had everything, except education. He admitted it and tried hard to convince young people of its importance. After explaining the whys and so forth, he would always end with this tale. He said that whenever he was at a party or some social gathering and the group at which he was standing would start an intelligent conversation, he would say, "Excuse me please" and then go to the men's room. As a result, he said he spent one third of his life going to the men's room, one third of it in the men's room, and one third coming back.

To be able to read and associate the meaning with the words read. Someone once said that education is the process by which a set of principles are driven down your throat. Right now all of you are debating this for yourself in your own minds. Some pro and some con. You see we can all decide for ourselves. We have that option. To think, to consider and then to debate, and arrive at a solution common to all.

"Where do we go from here?" that is what the band Chicago asked of you years back and that is what I am now asking. All of us are uniquely different and all of us have placed different values in different things. But there is one thing that is common to all of us at this particular moment in our lives. That is the will to embark on something new. Whether it is to pursue individual interests or college, we have got to have the attitude to win. Never consider anything too difficult.

Who was it who said it couldn't be done
But he with a chuckle replied, "Maybe it can't but I'll be one
Who won't say so until I've tried."
So he buckled right in with a bit of a grin
And if it hurt he didn't show it
He tackled the thing that couldn't be done
And he did it!

We have got to have this attitude and will to win. Never say die. Yeah it is going to be tough. The reward of something well done is to have done it. You've done it now what are you going to do with it?

That concludes my speech, but there is something I feel compelled to say and there isn't but one way to say it,

In my four years of attending LaGrange Senior High...I was damn proud to be a Granger!

June 1, 1973
Graduation Commencement Speech
John McHugh

We know what we are, but know not what we may be.
-Shakespeare

Potential-You are a weed but...you can become a rose.

> We are all weeds. Emerson said that a weed is a plant whose virtues have not yet been discovered.

Consult not your fears but your hopes and your dreams. Think not about your frustrations, but about your unfulfilled potential. Concern yourself not with what you tried and failed in, but with what it is still possible for you to do.
-Pope John XXIII

The only person you are destined to become is the person you decide to be.
-Ralph Waldo Emerson

There is no heavier burden than an unfulfilled potential.
-Charles Shultz

It's not what you've got; it's what you use that makes a difference.
-Zig Ziglar

Continuous effort - not strength or intelligence - is the key to unlocking our potential.
-Winston Churchill

Potential has a shelf life. -Margaret Atwood

First, say to yourself what you would be; and then do what you
have to do.
-Epictetus

There is no man living who isn't capable of doing more than he
thinks he can do.
-Henry Ford

I grew up like a neglected weed - ignorant of liberty, having no
experience of it.
-Harriet Tubman

The world is all gates, all opportunities, strings of tension
waiting to be struck.
-Ralph Waldo Emerson

It isn't where you came from; it's where you're going that counts.
-Ella Fitzgerald

I would have been able to free a thousand more slaves if I could
only have convinced them that they were slaves.
-Harriet Tubman

Life is a lively process of becoming.
-Douglas MacArthur

When you catch a glimpse of your potential, that's when passion
is born.
-Zig Ziglar

The big challenge is to become all that you have the possibility
of becoming. You cannot believe what it does to the human
spirit to maximize your human potential and stretch yourself to
the limit.
-Jim Rohn

You can't choose your potential, but you can choose to fulfill it.
-Theodore Roosevelt

Link yourself to your potential not to your past. -Stephen Covey

Ever since I was a child I have had this instinctive urge for expansion and growth. To me, the function and duty of a quality human being is the sincere and honest development of one's potential.
-Bruce Lee

Human potential is the only limitless resource we have in this world.
-Carly Fiorina

You have more potential than you think. -Sam Snead

Do you want to have an easy life? Then always stay with the herd and lose yourself in the herd.
-Friedrich Nietzsche

The most precious of all possessions is power over ourselves.
-John Locke

When the book "Gone with the Wind" was being written I was a four-dollar-a-day laborer in Oklahoma and not in anybody's mind for anything.
-Clark Gable

Death is not the greatest tragedy in life. The greatest tragedy is what dies inside us while we live. We need not fear death. We need fear only that we may exist without having sensed something of the possibilities that lie within human existence.
-Norman Cousins

Lilies that fester smell far worse than weeds.
-Shakespeare

For all sad words of tongue or pen,
The saddest are these: "It might have been."
-John Greenleaf Whittier

It's not about what it is; it's about what it can become.
-Dr. Seuss

In the long run, we shape our lives, and we shape ourselves. The process never ends until we die. And the choices we make are ultimately our own responsibility.
-Eleanor Roosevelt

Making Good Choices-Will
you stay a weed?

> *What we do now dictates whether we*
> *will be a weed the rest of our life.*

C arefully watch your thoughts, for they become your words. Manage and watch your words, for they will become your actions. Consider and judge your actions, for they have become your habits. Acknowledge and watch your habits, for they shall become your values. Understand and embrace your values, for they become your destiny.
-Mahatma Gandhi

You have brains in your head
You have feet in your shoes
You can steer yourself in any direction you choose!
-Dr. Seuss

See what you're doing wrong, laugh at it, change and do better.
-Spencer Johnson

Consider the postage stamp, my son. It secures success through its ability to stick to one thing till it gets there.
-Josh Billings

As in a game of cards, so in the game of life, we must play what is dealt to us, and the glory consists, not so much in winning, as in playing a poor hand well.
-Josh Billings

We are the creative force of our life, and through our own decisions rather than our conditions, if we carefully learn to do certain things, we can accomplish those goals.
-Stephen Covey

Choices are the hinges of destiny.
-Edwin Markham

The key to accepting responsibility for your life is to accept the fact that your choices, every one of them, are leading you inexorably to either success or failure, however you define those terms.
-Neal Boortz

You can measure a man's character by the choices he makes under pressure.
-Winston Churchill

One's philosophy is not best expressed in words; it is expressed in the choices one makes... and the choices we make are ultimately our responsibility.
-Eleanor Roosevelt

There's no such thing as work-life balance. There are work-life choices, and you make them, and they have consequences.
-Jack Welch

Elections belong to the people. It's their decision. If they decide to turn their back on the fire and burn their behinds, then they will just have to sit on their blisters.
-Abraham Lincoln

A smart girl leaves before she is left.
-Marilyn Monroe

My first guess is sometimes right. My second never is.
-J.P. Morgan

We made too many wrong mistakes. -Yogi Berra

If you could kick the person in the pants responsible for most of
your trouble, you wouldn't sit for a month.
-Theodore Roosevelt

The final forming of a person's character lies in their own hands.
-Anne Frank

When I was boxing I made five million and wound up broke,
owing the government a million.
-Joe Louis

The most important decisions you make are not the things you
do, but the things you decide not to do.
-Steve Jobs

My buddies wanted to be firemen, farmers or policemen,
something like that. Not me, I just wanted to steal people's
money!
-John Dillinger

Honor is simply the morality of superior men.
-H. L. Mencken

Your time is limited, so don't waste it living someone else's life.
Don't be trapped by dogma - which is living with the results of
other people's thinking. Don't let the noise of others' opinions
drown out your own inner voice. And most important, have the
courage to follow your heart and intuition.
-Steve Jobs

The more I think of it, the more I realize there are no answers.
Life is to be lived.
-Marilyn Monroe

I am not a product of my circumstances. I am a product of my
decisions. -Stephen Covey

Common sense is very uncommon.
-Horace Greeley

Our lives are a sum total of the choices we have made.
-Wayne Dyer

By taking responsibility for how you choose to respond to anything or anyone, you're aligning yourself with the beautiful dance of life.
-Wayne Dyer

Don't put all your eggs in one basket.
-Miguel de Cervantes

Our incomes are like our shoes; if too small, they gall and pinch us; but if too large, they cause us to stumble and to trip.
-John Locke

Things which matter most must never be at the mercy of things which matter least.
-Johann Wolfgang von Goethe

All that glitters is not gold.
-Shakespeare

What is right to be done cannot be done too soon.
-Jane Austen

Cutting negative people from my life does not mean I hate them, it simply means I respect me.
-Marilyn Monroe

If a man can beat you, walk him.
-Satchel Paige

Don't waste your love on somebody, who doesn't value it.
-William Shakespeare

You can never make the same mistake twice because the second time you make it, it's not a mistake, it's a choice.
-Steven Denn

We are our choices. -Jean-Paul Sartre

As is my custom, I was eating lunch in my car when a Paul Harvey "Rest of the Story" concerning marriage came on. He said that marriage has several stages beginning with the excitement of new love and then proceeds through the various changes that occur with time to both the marriage and the couple. He said that a marriage when the children are toddlers was different than the marriage when the children were in high school. As the situation of the marriage changes so too does the relationship and the necessity for adaptation. All of the above is common sense and wasn't news to me, but then he added something I hadn't considered and I am now offering to you as advice. Let's say you are in the seventh year of your marriage and you have two small children. You are not happy because the excitement you experienced in the early days of marriage is gone and replaced with dirty diapers. You decide you want a divorce. If you leave this marriage and remarry, the stages start over. In other words you may have children with the second spouse and then the diaper phase again begins to erode the excitement phase. You become unhappy again. In leaving the first marriage you did not have the opportunity to experience the succeeding phase of the marriage. Each phase, and there are about seven, has a different set of factors that in turn affect the marriage in different ways. So when you divorce, not only do you have to start the process over, you miss out on the potential benefits of your marriage having "earned" entry to the next phase. With each succeeding phase the marriage becomes stronger. This might be something to think about when you selfishly begin to wine about not being happy.

I was relating the Paul Harvey commentary to my wife of almost forty years. I was thinking about all the phases we had gone through and are still going through and trust me there can be more than seven. It dawned on me that one can only say "The best decision I ever made" if there has been a long period of time and decisions from which to consider. After some reflection, I said, "Karen, you are the best decision I have ever made."

Without a pause she quickly replied, "Considering some of the decisions you've made John that ain't saying much."

Before I could feign disappointment, I remembered losing all that money in a Ponzi scheme. All I could muster in response was, "Good point dear."

If you are working on something exciting that you really care about, you don't have to be pushed. The vision pulls you.
-Steve Jobs

The Power of Visualization-If you can conceive it you can achieve it.

> *Who wants to be a weed? Something that is not wanted and often discarded; a weed of society.*

L osers visualize the penalties of failure. Winners visualize the rewards of success.
-William S. Gilbert

If you want to be successful, it's just this simple. Know what you are doing. Love what you are doing. And believe in what you are doing.
-Will Rogers

I wanted you to see what real courage is, instead of getting the idea that courage is a man with a gun in his hand. It's when you know you're licked before you begin, but you begin anyway and see it through no matter what.
-Atticus Finch-*To Kill a Mockingbird*

If you are working on something exciting that you really care about, you don't have to be pushed. The vision pulls you.
-Steve Jobs

Envisioning the end is enough to put the means in motion.
-Dorothea Brande

Where there is no vision, there is no hope.
-George Washington Carver

Visualize this thing that you want, see it, feel it, believe in it.
Make your mental blue print, and begin to build.
-Robert Collier

You can't depend on your eyes when your imagination is out of
focus.
-Mark Twain

If you want to reach a goal, you must 'see the reaching' in your
own mind before you actually arrive at your goal.
-Zig Ziglar

Formulate and stamp indelibly on your mind a mental picture of
yourself as succeeding. Hold this picture tenaciously and never
permit it to fade. Your mind will seek to develop this picture!
-Dr. Norman Vincent Peale

Wishing will not bring riches. But desiring riches with a state of
mind that becomes an obsession, then planning definite ways
and means to acquire riches, and backing those plans with
persistence which does not recognize failure, will bring riches.
-Napoleon Hill

Everyone visualizes whether he knows it or not. Visualizing is
the great secret of success.
-Genevieve Behrend

Be not afraid of life. Believe that life is worth living, and your
belief will help create the fact.
-William James

Everything you can imagine is real. -Pablo Picasso

A man to carry on a successful business must have imagination.
He must see things as in a vision, a dream of the whole thing.
-Charles M. Schwab

When you expect things to happen - strangely enough - they do
happen.
-J.P. Morgan

The main trouble with despair is that it is self-fulfilling. People who fear the worst tend to invite it. Heads that are down can't scan the horizon for new openings. Bursts of energy do not spring from a spirit of defeat. Ultimately, helplessness leads to hopelessness.
-Norman Cousins

Imagination is more important than knowledge. For while knowledge defines all we currently know and understand, imagination points to all we might yet discover and create.
-Albert Einstein

The man who has no imagination has no wings.
-Muhammad Ali

All that we are is the result of what we have thought.
-Buddha

Vision without action is daydreaming and action without vision is a nightmare.
-Anonymous

To accomplish great things we must first dream, then visualize, then plan... believe... act!
-Alfred A. Montapert

The harder you work... and visualize something, the luckier you get.
-Seal

If you can dream it, you can do it. -Walt Disney

Nothing happens unless first a dream.
-Carl Sandburg

You will never be greater than the thoughts that dominate your mind. -Napoleon Hill

Logic will get you from A to B. Imagination will take you everywhere. -Albert Einstein

Ninety-nine percent of the failures come from
people who have the habit of making excuses.
-George Washington Carver

Responsibility-Take ownership in your future.

> *The decision is yours because the direction which you point your education will determine your future.*

This above all: to thine ownself be true.
-William Shakespeare

The moment you take responsibility for everything in your life is the moment you can change anything in your life.
-Hal Elrod

What lies behind you and what lies in front of you, pales in comparison to what lies inside of you.
-Ralph Waldo Emerson

Only I can change my life. No one can do it for me.
-Carol Burnett

When you make a mistake, there are only three things you should ever do about it: 1. Admit it. 2. Learn from it, and 3. Don't repeat it.
-Bear Bryant

How many cares one loses when one decides not to be something but to be someone.
-Gabrielle "Coco" Chanel

If you can't stand the heat, get out of the kitchen.
-Harry S. Truman

Happiness depends upon ourselves.
-Aristotle

A harmful truth is better than a useful lie.
-Thomas Mann

Go for it now. The future is promised to no one.
-Wayne Dyer

For they conquer who believe they can.
-John Dryden

There is nothing either good or bad but thinking makes it so.
-Shakespeare

We are made wise not by the recollection of our past, but by the
responsibility for our future.
-George Bernard Shaw

Leadership - leadership is about taking responsibility, not
making excuses.
-Mitt Romney

One's philosophy is not best expressed in words; it is expressed
in the choices one makes... and the choices we make are
ultimately our responsibility.
-Eleanor Roosevelt

Next to doing the right thing, the most important thing is to let
people know you are doing the right thing.
-John D. Rockefeller

The first thing (in credit) is character... before money or
anything else. Money cannot buy it.
-J.P. Morgan

I am good, but not an angel. I do sin, but I am not the devil. I am
pretty, but not beautiful. I have friends, but I am not the
peacemaker.
-Marilyn Monroe

Whatever happens, take responsibility.
-Tony Robbins

There is no growth except in the fulfilment of obligations.
-Antoine de Saint-Exupery

You cannot escape the responsibility of tomorrow by evading it today.
-Abraham Lincoln

Those who enjoy responsibility usually get it; those who merely like exercising authority usually lose it.
-Malcolm Forbes

Accountability breeds response-ability. -Stephen Covey

Action springs not from thought, but from a readiness for responsibility.
-Dietrich Bonhoeffer

Man must cease attributing his problems to his environment, and learn again to exercise his will - his personal responsibility.
-Albert Einstein

Responsibility is what awaits outside the Eden of Creativity.
-Nadine Gordimer

Rank does not confer power or privilege. It imposes responsibility.
-Peter Drucker

It is a painful thing to look at your own trouble and know that you yourself and no one else has made it.
-Sophocles

Never trouble another for what you can do for yourself.
-Thomas Jefferson

We can evade reality, but we cannot evade the consequences of evading reality. -Ayn Rand

The man that complains about the way a ball bounces is likely the one who dropped it. -Lou Holtz

Even if you're on the right track, you'll get run over if you just sit there.
-Will Rogers

Assign Goals-Reach a little further than your talents dictate.

> Assign goals that reach a little further than
> your talents dictate and pursue them.

A dream is just a dream. A goal is a dream with a plan and a deadline.
-Harvey MacKay

What you get by achieving your goals is not as important as what you become by achieving your goals.
-Zig Ziglar

Plans are of little importance, but planning is essential.
-Winston Churchill

Someone's sitting in the shade today because someone planted a tree a long time ago.
-Warren Buffett

Setting goals is the first step in turning the invisible into the visible.
-Tony Robbins

When it is obvious that the goals cannot be reached, don't adjust the goals, adjust the action steps.
-Confucius

Life takes on meaning when you become motivated, set goals and charge after them in an unstoppable manner.
-Les Brown

Review your goals twice every day in order to be focused on
achieving them.
-Les Brown

Success is a science; if you have the conditions, you get the
result.
-Oscar Wilde

Happiness is not a goal; it is a by-product.
-Eleanor Roosevelt

Success is nearest to those whose efforts are intense and sincere.
-Patanjali

If you want to be happy, set a goal that commands your
thoughts, liberates your energy and inspires your hopes.
-Andrew Carnegie

Our goals can only be reached through a vehicle of a plan, in
which we must fervently believe, and upon which we must
vigorously act. There is no other route to success.
-Pablo Picasso

A goal properly set is halfway reached.
-Zig Ziglar

The rung of a ladder was never meant to rest upon, but only to
hold a man's foot long enough to enable him to put the other
somewhat higher.
-Thomas Henry Huxley

Plan your work-work your plan.
-Anonymous

If your only goal is to become rich, you will never achieve it.
-John D. Rockefeller

If you're bored with life-you don't get up every morning with a
burning desire to do things-you don't have enough goals.
-Lou Holtz

21

There is nothing noble in being superior to your fellow man; true nobility is being superior to your former self.
-Ernest Hemingway

Self-Improvement-Be a better version of yourself.

> *In this way you will realize your goals and in turn you will have bettered yourself. Everyone must better himself.*

M ake the most of yourself....for that is all there is of you.
-Ralph Waldo Emerson

You can never be overdressed or overeducated.
-Oscar Wilde

Formal education will make you a living; self-education will make you a fortune.
-Jim Rohn

When you see a good person, think of becoming like her/him. When you see someone not so good, reflect on your own weak points.
-Confucius

Attack the evil that is within yourself, rather than attacking the evil that is in others.
-Confucius

To live is the rarest thing in the world. Most people exist, that is all.
-Oscar Wilde

A quitter never wins and a winner never quits. -Napoleon Hill

There are no traffic jams on the extra mile.
-Zig Ziglar

There is no need for me continuing unless I'm able to improve.
-Knute Rockne

Do one thing every day that scares you.
-Eleanor Roosevelt

The unexamined life is not worth living. -Socrates

We are what we repeatedly do. Excellence, then, is not an act,
but a habit -Aristotle

I count him braver who overcomes his desires than him who
conquers his enemies; for the hardest victory is over self.
-Aristotle

Never look back unless you are planning to go that way.
-Henry David Thoreau

Get the better of yourself - this is the best kind of victory.
-Miguel de Cervantes

Truth isn't always beauty, but the hunger for it is.
-Nadine Gordimer

Be so busy improving yourself that you have no time to criticize
others.
-Anonymous

Don't compare yourself to others. Compare yourself to the
person from yesterday.
-Anonymous

Those who cannot change their minds cannot change anything.
-George Bernard Shaw

The question isn't who is going to let me; it is who is going to
stop me? -Ayn Rand

*We all have dreams. But in order to make
dreams come into reality, it takes an awful lot
of determination, dedication, self-discipline,
and effort.*
-Jesse Owens

Discipline-Part of success is just showing up.

> One is naïve to rationalize that one can wait for developments because there is not that much time. Time waits for no man and you are no exception so act now.

It was character that got us out of bed, commitment that moved us into action and discipline that enabled us to follow through.
-Zig Ziglar

Either you run the day, or the day runs you.
-John Rohn

Would you have a great empire? Rule over yourself.
-Publilius Syrus

Procrastination is opportunity's assassin.
-Victor Kiam

It is safer to search in the maze than to remain in a cheese-less situation.
-Spencer Johnson

Discipline is the bridge between goals and accomplishment.
-John Rohn

The surest test of discipline is its absence.
-Clara Barton

We first make our habits, and then our habits make us.
-John Dryden

If we keep doing what we're doing, we're going to keep getting
what we're getting.
-Stephen Covey

The people you surround yourself with influence your behaviors,
so choose friends who have healthy habits.
-Dan Buettner

Beware the fury of a patient man.
-John Dryden

To be without some of the things you want is an indispensable
part of happiness.
-Anonymous

You cannot push any one up a ladder unless he be willing to
climb a little himself.
-Andrew Carnegie

Giving should be entered into in just the same way as investing.
Giving is investing.
-John D. Rockefeller

Effective leadership is putting first things first. Effective
management is discipline, carrying it out.
-Steven Covey

The only discipline that lasts is self-discipline.
-Bum Phillips

Discipline yourself and others won't have to.
-John Wooden

Good habits formed at youth make all the difference.
-Aristotle

No man is free who is not master of himself. -Epictetus

Self-discipline is doing what needs to be done when it needs to
be done even when you don't feel like doing it.
-Anonymous

I could only achieve success in my life through self-discipline,
and I applied it until my wish and my will became one.
-Nikola Tesla

The profile of a wealthy person is this hard work, perseverance,
and most of all, self-discipline.
-Zig Ziglar

I count him braver who overcomes his desires than him who
conquers his enemies; for the hardest victory is over self.
-Aristotle

A nail is driven out by another nail; habit is overcome by habit.
- Erasmus

Just do it! First you make your habits, then your habits make
you!
-Lucas Remmerswaal

Discipline not desire determines your destiny.
-Anonymous

Compassion, tolerance, forgiveness and a sense of self-discipline
are qualities that help us lead our daily lives with a calm mind.
-Dalai Lama

I am always asked, "What's the secret to success?" There are no
secrets. Be humble. Be hungry. And always be the hardest
worker in the room.
-Dwayne Johnson

The ability to discipline yourself to delay gratification in the
short term in order to enjoy greater rewards in the long term is
the indispensable prerequisite for success.
-Maxwell Maltz

No good decision was ever made in a swivel chair.
-Patton

Be Decisive-Act!

> *Decide. Decide what you want to do. Align your decisions with your capabilities and pursue it. Put together all that school has given you and make it work.*

A good plan, violently executed now, is better than a perfect plan next week.
-General Patton

Chaotic action is preferable to orderly inaction.
-Will Rogers

Study without desire spoils the memory, and it retains nothing that it takes in.
-Leonardo da Vinci

When obstacles arise, you change your direction to reach your goal; you do not change your decision to get there.
-Zig Ziglar

Don't find fault, find a remedy.
-Henry ford

The base paths belonged to me, the runner. The rules gave me the right. I always went into a bag full speed, feet first. I had sharp spikes on my shoes. If the baseman stood where he had no business to be and got hurt, that was his fault.
-Ty Cobb

The journey of a thousand miles begins with one step.
-Lao Tzu

I hear and I forget. I see and I remember. I do and I understand.
-Confucius

Well done is better than well said.
-Benjamin Franklin

Let him that would move the world first move himself.
-Socrates

I'll tell you what bravery really is. Bravery is just determination
to do a job that you know has to be done.
-Audie Murphy

To go forward you have to leave something behind.
-Steve Jobs

Be miserable. Or motivate yourself. Whatever has to be done, it's
always your choice.
-Wayne Dyer

It is not enough to have intuitions; we must act on them; we
must live them.
-Patanjali

You can't build a reputation on what you are going to do.
-Henry Ford

Whatever you can do or dream you can, begin it. Boldness has
genius, power, and magic in it.
-Johann Wolfgang von Goethe

Action may not always bring happiness; but there is no
happiness without action.
-Benjamin Disraeli

Act boldly and unseen forces will come to your aid.
-Dorothea Brande

All the beautiful sentiments in the world weigh less than a single
lovely action. -James Russell Lowell

John C. McHugh M.D.

Man's greatness consists in his ability to do and the proper application of his powers to things needed to be done.
-Frederick Douglass

Man who waits for roast duck to fly into his mouth must wait very, very long time.
-Chinese Proverb

The sluggard buries his hand in the dish; He is weary of bringing it to his mouth again.
-Proverbs 26:15

When I have business on hand I think it is better to have it done quickly. -J.P. Morgan

We cannot do everything at once, but we can do something at once. -Calvin Coolidge

Do not be like the cat who wanted a fish but was afraid to get his paws wet.
-William Shakespeare

The majority see the obstacles; the few see the objectives; history records the successes of the latter, while oblivion is the reward of the former.
-Alfred Armand Montapert

After all is said and done, more is said than done.
-American Proverb

God says, "Rise and I will rise with you." He does not say, "Sleep and I will sleep with you."
-Arabian Proverb

Apply yourself. Get all the education you can, but then, by God, do something. Don't just stand there, make it happen.
-Lee Iacocca

The wise man does at once what the fool does finally.
-Machiavelli

Science may have found a cure for most evils;
but it has found no remedy for the worst of
them all - the apathy of human beings.
-Helen Keller

Apathy-The deadly art of not caring.

> *Block out apathy and it constituents*

The worst sin toward our fellow creatures is not to hate them, but to be indifferent to them: that's the essence of inhumanity.
-George Bernard Shaw

Willpower is the key to success. Successful people strive no matter what they feel by applying their will to overcome apathy, doubt or fear.
-Dan Millman

Apathy can be overcome by enthusiasm, and enthusiasm can only be aroused by two things: first, an ideal, with takes the imagination by storm, and second, a definite intelligible plan for carrying that ideal into practice.
-Arnold Toynbee

Is it ignorance or apathy? Hey, I don't know and I don't care.
-Jimmy Buffett

Apathy is a sort of living oblivion.
-Horace Greeley

The road to hell is paved with good intentions.
-Samuel Johnson

Knowing is not enough; we must apply. Willing is not enough; we must do.
-Johann Wolfgang von Goethe

The price of apathy towards public affairs is to be ruled by evil
men.
-Plato

There can be no transforming of darkness into light and of
apathy into movement without emotion.
-Carl Jung

Apathy is a sort of living oblivion.
-Horace Greeley

Tolerance it a tremendous virtue, but the immediate neighbors
of tolerance are apathy and weakness.
-James Goldsmith

By far the most dangerous foe we have to fight is apathy-
indifference from whatever cause, not from a lack of knowledge,
but from carelessness, from absorption in other pursuits, from a
contempt bred of self satisfaction.
-William Osler

Such has often been my apathy, when objects long sought, and
earnestly desired, were placed within my reach.
-Nathaniel Hawthorne

If moderation is a fault, then indifference is a crime.
-Jack Kerouac

The world will not be destroyed by those who do evil, but by
those who watch them without doing anything
-Albert Einstein

...so much attention is paid to the aggressive sins, such as
violence and cruelty, and greed with all their tragic effects, that
too little attention is paid to the passive sins, such as apathy and
laziness, which in the long run can have a more devastating and
destructive effect upon society than the others.
-Eleanor Roosevelt

Most human beings have an almost infinite capacity for taking things for granted.
-Aldous Huxley

There is nothing harder than the softness of indifference.
-Juan Montalvo

People who are unable to motivate themselves must be content with mediocrity, no matter how impressive their other talents.
-Andrew Carnegie

To win takes a complete commitment of mind and body. When you can't make that commitment, they don't call you a champion anymore.
-Rocky Marciano

A person may cause evil to others not only by his actions but by his inaction, and in either case he is justly accountable to them for the injury.
-John Stuart Mill

Some men go through the forest and see no firewood.
-English Proverb

The opposite of love is not hate, it's indifference. The opposite of art is not ugliness, it's indifference. The opposite of faith is not heresy, it's indifference. And the opposite of life is not death, it's indifference.
-Elie Wiesel

History will have to record that the greatest tragedy of this period of social transition was not the strident clamor of the bad people, but the appalling silence of the good people.
-Martin Luther King, Jr.

Find out just what any people will quietly submit to and you have the exact measure of the injustice and wrong which will be imposed on them.
-Fredrick Douglas

I'm trying to find myself. Sometimes that's not easy.
-Marilyn Monroe

Believe in Yourself-Whether you think you can or can't...you're right.

> *Counter with a concern for yourself.*

No one can make you feel inferior without your consent.
-Eleanor Roosevelt

Everybody has goals, aspirations or whatever, and everybody has been at a point in their life where nobody believed in them.
-Eminem

Don't let someone else's opinion of you become your reality.
-Les Brown

Doing what you love is the cornerstone of having abundance in your life.
-Wayne Dyer

Would you have a great empire? Rule over yourself.
-Publilius Syrus

It matters not what you are thought to be, but what you are.
-Publilius Syrus

The higher we soar the smaller we appear to those who cannot fly.
-Friedrich Nietzsche

All I need to make a comedy is a park, a policeman and a pretty girl. -Charlie Chaplin

We are all about the same in the beginning. We have about the same amount of instincts, desires, and capabilities. It is up to us whether we keep them alive or not. I don't believe anybody was ever born mean or pessimistic or under-privileged. We all have the seed of greatness within us. I know I'm no better than anybody else. I've had pretty good luck and good health and I've learned to keep plugging away
-Clark Gable

No matter what happens, always be yourself. -Dale Carnegie

It is in our darkest moments that we must focus to see the light.
-Aristotle

You must learn to be still in the midst of activity and to be vibrantly alive in repose.
-Indira Gandhi

Do not pray for an easy life, pray for the strength to endure a difficult one. -Bruce Lee

If you are not in the process of becoming the person you want to be, you are automatically engaged in becoming the person you don't want to be.
-Dale Carnegie

It isn't what you have, or who you are, or where you are, or what you are doing that makes you happy or unhappy. It is what you think about.
-Dale Carnegie

To find yourself, think for yourself. -Socrates

Not to be cheered by praise, not to be grieved by blame, but to know thoroughly one's own virtues or powers are the characteristics of an excellent man.
-Satchel Paige

Nothing is impossible, the word itself says, "I'm possible."
-Audrey Hepburn

John C. McHugh M.D.

Age is a case of mind over matter. If you don't mind, it don't matter.
-Satchel Paige

If you can dream it, you can achieve it.
-Zig Ziglar

There is nothing either good or bad but thinking makes it so.
-William Shakespeare

When one must, one can. For it is by hunger.
-Yiddish Proverb

It is not in the stars to hold our destiny but in ourselves.
-William Shakespeare

It is never too late to be what you might have been.
-George Eliot

I can be changed by what happens to me. But I refuse to be reduced by it. -Maya Angelou

I don't measure a man's success by how high he climbs but how high he bounces when he hits bottom.
-George S. Patton

I will not let anyone walk through my mind with their dirty feet.
-Mahatma Gandhi

You must expect great things of yourself before you can do them.
-Michael Jordan

If you make friends with yourself you'll never be alone.
-Maxwell Maltz

Don't be distracted by criticism. Remember - the only taste of success some people have is when they take a bite out of you.
-Zig Ziglar

The mind is everything. What you think you become. -Buddha

*Anybody can become angry - that is easy, but
to be angry with the right person and to the
right degree and at the right time and for the
right purpose, and in the right way - that is not
within everybody's power and is not easy.
-Aristotle*

41

Equanimity-Keeping your cool.

The pressure is on.

K eep your head when all about you are losing theirs and blaming it on you.
-Rudyard Kipling

You always own the option of having no opinion. There is never any need to get worked up or to trouble your soul about things you can't control. These things are not asking to be judged by you. Leave them alone.
-Marcus Aurelius

Be cool at the equator; keep thy blood fluid at the Pole.
-Herman Melville

Even a happy life cannot be without a measure of darkness, and the word happy would lose its meaning if it were not balanced by sadness. It is far better take things as they come along with patience and equanimity.
-Carl Jung

Equanimity is calamity's medicine.
-Publilius Syrus

What is patience but an equanimity which enables you to rise superior to the trials of life.
-William Osler

I'll tell you how I handle stress. I say-This too shall pass. You've got to try to stay cool and admit when you're wrong, and tell them when you're right.
-Helen Thomas

For want of self-restraint many men are engaged all their lives in fighting with difficulties of their own making, and rendering success impossible by their own cross-grained ungentleness; whilst others, it may be much less gifted, make their way and achieve success by simple patience, equanimity, and self-control.
-Samuel Smiles

When force of circumstance upsets your equanimity lose no time in recovering your self-control, and do not remain out of tune longer than you can help. Habitual recurrence to the harmony will increase your mastery of it.
-Marcus Aurelius

Happy is the man who can endure the highest and lowest fortune. He who has endured such vicissitudes with equanimity has deprived misfortune of its power.
-Seneca

Philosophy teaches us to bear with equanimity the misfortunes of others.
-Oscar Wilde

No doubt you are right... there would be far less suffering amongst mankind if men... did not employ their imaginations so assiduously in recalling the memory of past sorrow, instead of bearing their present lot with equanimity.
-Johann Wolfgang von Goethe

The two Virtues of Equanimity and Compassion become more available to the person whose ego-shell has been smashed-either by great suffering or by great love-or by both.
-Richard Rohr

If your stomach disputes you, lie down and pacify it with cool thoughts.
-Satchel Paige

If a man amounts to much in this world, he must encounter many and varied annoyances whose number mounts as his effectiveness increases. -Grace Coolidge

I don't worry about stress. I create it. -James Mattis

At a cardiac arrest, the first procedure is to take your own pulse.
-Samuel Shem

He who keeps his cool best wins.
-Norman Cousins

For a righteous man falls seven times and rises again, but the wicked are overthrown by calamity.
-Proverbs 24:16

What a man needs is not courage but nerve control, cool headedness. This he can get only by practice.
-Theodore Roosevelt

Men are disturbed not by things, but by the view which they take of them.
-Epictetus

A son can bear with equanimity the loss of his father, but the loss of his inheritance may drive him to despair.
-Machiavelli

A truly brave man is ever serene; he is never taken by surprise; nothing ruffles the equanimity of his spirit. In the heat of battle he remains cool; in the midst of catastrophes he keeps level his mind. Earthquakes do not shake him, he laughs at storms.
-Inazo Nitobe

Gratitude, not understanding, is the secret to joy and equanimity.
-Anne Lamott

If your opponent is of a choleric temper, irritate him.
-Sun Tzu

Change what cannot be accepted and accept what cannot be changed.
- Reinhold Niebuhr

*At times our own light goes out and is
rekindled by a spark from another person.
Each of us has cause to think with deep
gratitude of those who have lighted the flame
within us.*
-Albert Schweitzer

Gratitude/Loyalty/Respect-
You are standing on the shoulders of others.

> *You have the task of fulfilling the dreams of those who love you.*

N one of us got to where we are alone. Whether the assistance we received was obvious or subtle, acknowledging someone's help is a big part of understanding the importance of saying thank you.
-Harvey Mackay

You can get everything in life you want if you will just help enough other people get what they want. -Zig Ziglar

Talk to someone about themselves and they'll listen for hours.
-Dale Carnegie

Honesty and integrity are by far the most important assets of an entrepreneur. -Zig Ziglar

Every time we remember to say thank you, we experience nothing less than heaven on earth.
-Sarah Ban Breathnach

Take time to be kind and to say 'thank you.' -Zig Ziglar

Being deeply loved by someone gives you strength, while loving someone deeply gives you courage. -Lao Tzu

We make a living by what we get, but we make a life by what
we give.
-Winston Churchill

No act of kindness no matter how small is ever wasted.
-Aesop

I've learned that people will forget what you said, people will
forget what you did, but people will never forget how you made
them feel.
-Maya Angelou

Without kindness there can be no true joy.
-Thomas Carlyle

What I spent, I had; what I kept, I lost; what I gave, I have.
-Henry Ward Beecher

All cruelty springs from weakness.
-Seneca

After I hit a home run I had a habit of running the bases with my
head down. I figured the pitcher already felt bad enough without
me showing him up rounding the bases.
-Mickey Mantle

A champion owes everybody something. He can never pay back
for all the help he got, for making him an idol.
-Jack Dempsey

True friends stab you in the front.
-Oscar Wilde

There are two days in the year that we cannot do anything,
yesterday and tomorrow.
-Mahatma Gandhi

Gratitude is the healthiest of all human emotions. The more you
express gratitude for what you have, the more likely you will
have even more to express gratitude for. -Zig Ziglar

John C. McHugh M.D.

When you practice gratefulness, there is a sense of respect toward others. -Dalai Lama

Gratitude makes sense of our past, brings peace for today, and creates a vision for tomorrow.
-Melody Beattie

I follow three rules: Do the right thing, do the best you can, and always show people you care. You've got to make a sincere attempt to have the right goals to begin with, then go after them with appropriate effort, and remember that you can't really achieve anything great without the help of others.
-Lou Holtz

I've given no thought to whether I make friends fast or slowly. I don't have a lot of friends; I do have a lot of acquaintances. Friends are something else.
-Clark Gable

I'm selfish, impatient and a little insecure. I make mistakes, I am out of control and at times hard to handle. But if you can't handle me at my worst, then you sure as hell don't deserve me at my best.
-Marilyn Monroe

To have a friend you have to be a friend.
-Ralph Waldo Emerson

Some people give and forgive; other get and forget.
-Anonymous

I can no other answer make, but, thanks, and thanks.
-William Shakespeare

If I have seen further than others, it is by standing upon the shoulders of giants.
-Isaac Newton

Success is the result of perfection, hard work, learning from failure, loyalty, and persistence. -Colin Powell

You give loyalty, you'll get it back. You give love, you'll get it back.
-Tommy Lasorda

I'll take fifty percent efficiency to get one hundred percent loyalty.
-Samuel Goldwyn

You've got to give loyalty down, if you want loyalty up.
-Donald T. Regan

You can easily judge the character of a man by how he treats those who can do nothing for him.
-Johann Wolfgang von Goethe

You stand up for your teammates. Your loyalty is to them. You protect them through good and bad, because they'd do the same for you.
-Yogi Berra

Do a little more than you're paid to. Give a little more than you have to. Try a little harder than you want to. Aim a little higher than you think possible, and give a lot of thanks to God for health, family, and friends.
-Art Linkletter

Piglet noticed that even though he had a Very Small Heart, it could hold a rather large amount of Gratitude.
-Winnie-the-Pooh

A word of kindness is better than a fat pie.
-Russian Proverb

The ability to deal with people is as purchasable a commodity as sugar or coffee and I will pay more for that ability than for any other under the sun. -John D. Rockefeller

New friends may be poems but old friends are alphabets. Don't forget the alphabets because you will need them to read the poems. -Shakespeare

Gratitude is the most passionate transformative force in the cosmos.
-Sarah Ban Breathnach

We suffer a lot the few things we lack and we enjoy too little the many things we have.
-William Shakespeare

Don't trust the person who has broken faith once.
-William Shakespeare

Gratitude is the fairest blossom which springs from the soul.
-Henry Ward Beecher

A hundred times a day I remind myself that my inner and outer life depend on the labors of other men, living and dead, and that I must exert myself in order to give in the measure as I have received and am still receiving.
-Albert Einstein

When I started counting my blessings, my whole life turned around.
-Willie Nelson

Animals are reliable, many full of love, true in their affections, predictable in their actions, grateful and loyal. Difficult standards for people to live up to.
-Alfred Armand Montapert

Cultivate the habit of being grateful for every good thing that comes to you, and to give thanks continuously. And because all things have contributed to your advancement, you should include all things in your gratitude.
-Ralph Waldo Emerson

Regard your soldiers as your children and they will follow you into the deepest valleys; look on them as your own beloved sons, and they will stand by you even unto death.
-Sun Tzu

Cooper Davis

M y maternal grandfather, Robert Cooper Davis, was one
of about ten siblings born in LaGrange in a house very
near the Chattahoochee River just south of the city. He
attended college at North Georgia College in Dahlonega,
Georgia. The 1907 year book states that of all the freshmen,
Cooper Davis was by far the best football player and the best
dancer. After his freshman year, he transferred to the University
of Georgia and was on the 1909 football team, then known as the
Red and Blacks. I believe he then served in War World I in the
Navy. After the war, he obtained his Pharmacy degree at the
University of Georgia and then returned to LaGrange. After
working for an older pharmacist for several years, he started his
own business on the square in downtown LaGrange. He owned
Davis Pharmacy until the 1950's and when we moved to
LaGrange in 1969, the pharmacy was still in business and the
new owner kept the name. That building on the corner of the
square and the Davis name emblazoned on the front was always
a source of pride for me.

I really don't remember my grandfather, as he died when I was about four. I do remember at age three my walking from his home two blocks away to the pharmacy without the knowledge of my mother or grandmother. When I walked into the door I am told that my grandfather wanted to know where my mother was and when he determined I was alone he called the house. "Jennie, guess who just walked into the pharmacy?"

One may wonder why I'd include someone whom I hardly knew as someone very important in my life. Au contraire! You have to imagine my situation. My father had had an affair, a child, and divorced my mother. During the divorce proceedings, which was more akin to my mother being on trial, my father's attorney called me to the witness stand. I was in seventh grade. He tried to make me say disparaging things about my mother, which I did not do no matter how hard he tried or by rephrasing the questions. He lined up various bottles of different makes of bourbon on the table where he and my father were sitting.

"John, have you seen these bottles before?" the attorney asked me.

I had seen all them and many more like them before and then answered, "No I haven't."

"These are bottles that have been found in your mother's apartment. You have never seen these before?"

Without any hesitation, remorse or fear of lying, I said defiantly, "I have never seen them before. Butch probably put them there. He drinks more than my mother does anyway."

I preferred not to refer to my father as father or dad, his nickname was Butch and I used it as a derogatory insult to him. My mother's attorney, who my grandmother had paid five hundred dollars to represent us, then rose and approached the judge. After this discussion they all agreed to take me off the stand. I remember enjoying being up there. I had such disdain for Butch that testifying against him was gratifying. I think our attorney was beginning to think that if my line of testimony continued that neither my mother nor Butch would get the children. I also believe our attorney probably advised my mother that by allowing Butch to get the two under aged children, that being my little brother Jeff and I, would be better than us ending up in a foster home. So that was the verdict, Jeff and I were ordered to live with Butch. Mother was allowed to have the two of us one weekend a month. In retrospect, I feel that Butch went through all of the divorce proceedings to limit any responsibility for child support or alimony and to accomplish this he made my mother appear to the court as an unfit parent.

We had to live with my father for about a year and a half. Once every month like clockwork, mother showed up on Friday and we drove to LaGrange and then back to Smyrna that Sunday. Whereas where we lived in Smyrna was a business converted into a house, was cold and having no emotional connectivity to Butch and his "Huzzy" as my grandmother referred to her, the home in LaGrange was warm and had my mother and grandmother. It was great to get to LaGrange and horrible to have to go back to Smyrna. Standing there and seeing mother drive off and knowing it would be a month before she returned still bothers me.

When Butch decided he was going to move to Alaska he then no longer needed Jeff and me and so on one occasion when mother picked us up she was told she did not have to bring us back. Packing was very easy as I wanted no memory of the place and we departed never to return. After that day, I only saw my father once for about five minutes when I was working in a Belk's store during Christmas break in college. He just appeared without warning. I was as cold to him then as I had been when I had to live with him.

"Are your grades good?" he asked.

"I have a 3.85 GPA," I said.

"I had a 4.0 GPA at Auburn," he said.

"I am working. Good bye," I said. I never saw or spoke to him again and never had a desire to. Don't get me wrong, it is not a vengeance thing or an unwillingness to forgive. He just had not been a part of my life since seventh grade and my remembrance of him and the bad things he did was not pleasant. He just didn't exist to me.

My point is that although I don't remember my grandfather, he was the father I never had. He was someone who was a leader in the community, popular, athletic, and successful in his business. He was a deacon in the Presbyterian Church, which was across the street from his house. He did, however, struggle with alcoholism.

So, when we moved to LaGrange and someone would ask me who I was, I'd say, "John McHugh. My grandfather was Robert Cooper Davis. He was the pharmacist who owned Davis Pharmacy on the square." I never mentioned his name that someone did not say they knew him or that their father knew and liked him. Cooper Davis was friends with the early doctors in town. He went to Georgia games with them, he played golf with them at the Highlands Country Club in LaGrange, and they came to his pharmacy to eat lunch. To be friends with important people or to be a member of a country club was foreign to my family. I loved making the association. When I worked as an orderly at the hospital a lot of the patients I bathed would know him. I'd ask them to tell me what they knew of him and revelled in their stories. When I'd get home I'd repeat what I had heard and grandmother would embellish it. One of the stories had to do with my grandfather going to the Sugar Bowl in the 1940's by train with friends and returning with a crumpled hat and missing one of the men who had gone. He showed up in LaGrange days later. Nothing was said but much implied about his returning days later with no explanation.

What Robert Cooper Davis did for me was to give my mother legitimacy and in doing that gave me a sense of self worth. I was reminded of this every time I passed his drug store. It is no accident that he attended North Georgia College in 1907 and that I too enrolled there. I have his Pharmacy diploma, I purchased his home in LaGrange, I've named a child Cooper, and I have the chair he died in. The chair was in the front room of the house by a door. Grandmother said she heard him say "Bess" and when she got there he was slumped over and had died peacefully.

He was such a powerful influence that my mother felt his dying left a void of maleness in our family and that my father then began to act out having only women and children to answer to. Weak men do that.

Finally, to show the lasting influence he had on our lives long after his death, I'll relate something my grandmother did. One of her grandchildren got in trouble at school and the offense was such that one of "Jennie's boys" was kicked off the team. The particular coach was an imposing man and had coached with success at LaGrange High for many years. Without any hesitation or fear my seventy five year old ninety pound grandmother had my mother drive her to the coach's house to discuss the matter. She walked up to the house in her cotton summer dress sporting her small blue pocketbook and knocked on the front door while mother waited in the car.

"Now you listen here," she said using his first name. "My husband Cooper helped you get this job when you came to town and he supported you when you needed him. I want my grandson back on the team!"

After two weeks of running laps before and after practice Bess's grandson was back on the team.

Don't mess with Bess.

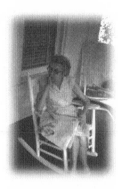

Bessie Clay

M y mother was flawed but otherwise perfect. No, I have not misspoken; however, I will explain when I get to her. My grandmother's life was dramatically affected by both a husband and a daughter who were alcoholics. It is sad when viewed in retrospect for someone having lived through a spouse's addiction only to then have to deal with a daughter as well. Not only were my grandmother, her house, and her savings there for us after my father left us, she was there for my mother her entire married life. My mother was a binge alcoholic and as a result, she had an "episode" about three times a year. When they occurred, they were bad, very bad. To my knowledge, her issues with alcohol began in the early sixties and may have indeed been caused by the death of her father in 1959. With each episode, my father became more and more inappropriate in his dealings with my mother. I will leave it at that; even though my mother passed away over twenty-five years ago, I am unable to speak of or write of my father's behavior towards my mother. I know we speak of the importance of forgiveness, but God may have given me too high a mountain on this one. Having said that, using as many euphemisms as possible, the following is a common scenario and why my grandmother was so important in my life.

My first memory of the problems starting was in our home on a dirt road in Columbus, Georgia, Norris Circle. Mother would drink to the point of being incapacitated, my father would do something very bad to her, and the next day we'd put her in the car and take her to meet my grandmother and aunt. I was in the second grade at St. Anne-Pacelli Catholic School at that time. The drop off point was usually a half way point at an elementary school parking lot in Pine Mountain, Georgia. I played on the school's playground as the details of the exchange were discussed. She would be taken to LaGrange for about two weeks while my grandmother nursed her to health and then we'd repeat the reverse process to get her back to Columbus. My mother would be to me the most perfect mother in the world...until it happened again. It usually happened on holidays, with the Christmas season being the worst. Over the years, and with each occurrence, my father's reaction became more severe and inappropriate. Each time, my grandmother was called and dutifully took care of the situation. On some occasions, and I don't know why, grandmother would come to our house to stay for a couple of weeks to nurse her, do the house cleaning, and to cook. It hurts me to this day that she had to cook for the son in law who each time had done things, which if we had had the where with all, would have landed him in jail. This continued throughout my childhood while my father was around and then continued when we moved in with grandmother in LaGrange after my father moved to Alaska. In LaGrange there was no Butch, but a heightened sense that people would find out why she was out of commission for days on end or that in her attempt to obtain alcohol, she'd get into legal trouble. We would find and destroy bottles of alcohol, we'd hide the keys to her car, or disconnect the distributor cap wiring so the car would not crank. We kept vigil on her in the house to keep her from leaving, something she detested. I learned very quickly the harsh language my mother must have learned in the Coast Guard during War World II.

Throughout all of this, my grandmother stood strong, financially supported my family, cooked, bought our school clothes, and continued to make our house a home. She was our stability when everything was out of whack.

When mother was all right, she was wonderful. She and grandmother shopped and cooked together. During the normal times what I experienced would be considered a very normal existence, with a loving mother and grandmother serving as our means of income between mother's usually short lived jobs.

57

Grandmother supported my mother when, at age fifty-five, she went back to college and earned her degree from Huntingdon College in Montgomery, some thirty years after dropping out of Huntingdon to join the Coast Guard. This involved a one hundred and eighty mile commute several times a week to get the degree and my mother loved the experience, the drive, the professors, and the friends she made. Grandmother made all of this possible. Mother received her degree the same year I graduated from High School.

My father leaving was the best thing that could have ever happened to both my mother and grandmother. Mother got the support of the LaGrange extended family and my grandmother had a rebirth of sorts. One minute she was living a quiet life alone and the next a daughter and five boys ranging from college age to third grade were coming in and out at a busying pace. Grandmother was fond of saying exasperatingly, "Jennie your children are making this house a thoroughfare!" She had to adapt and I feel our showing up helped her stay young and be a more active person. In addition, moving in with her allowed all of us the opportunity to know her better. I became as close to my grandmother as I was with my mother.

Grandmother came in handy on many fronts. When I was a senior in high school, I was supposed to have read *The Scarlet Letter* and give an oral report on it in English class. I wasn't much of the reader at that time, failed to read the book, and was due one morning to give the report. I asked grandmother if she had read the book and she said she had but that she did not remember much about it. She did say however that she had very close friend who was a retired English teacher and she could call her. My grandmother said, "John you get on the other line and I'll ask all the questions about the book and you listen in on the other line and take notes."

"Mary Louise, this is Bess Davis, how are you?"

"I am fine Bess and hope you are."

"Fine, fine I am just fine. Mary Louise I was just thinking about Hawthorne's *The Scarlet Letter* and was wondering if you remember the gist of it?"

"Oh, I do very much, I taught that book several years running. I know it like the back of my hand. Why do you ask?"

Taking the list of topics on which the report was to be based, my grandmother began asking her friend specifics regarding each. "I was wondering Mary Louise, what is the overall plot and theme of the book?" As grandmother's friend began to answer a large variety of questions, I was on the other line writing all the answers down. Grandmother continued, "That is very interesting, I don't think I remember that aspect of the story. Why do you feel Mary Louise that the story has relevance in today's culture?" My grandmother was way too good at this art of deception. It was if she had had to use this technique possibly as a student herself, I thought to myself at the time. After all the questions had been addressed beautifully by both my grandmother and her friend, the conversation ended.

"How was that John? Do you think that will work?"

"Perfect grandmother, I have enough now to easily regurgitate what she said to do my oral report." I continued, "Grandmother, were you a good student?"

"Heavens no, I was not and I absolutely hated Math. In fact John, I went to the Women's Normal School in Athens to be a teacher. At the end of my freshman year, two interesting things happened to me. I was given an "A" for a class in which I had made a "C" and I decided not to say anything about it. Then when the report cards came out that summer I had been mistakenly promoted to the junior class and I didn't say anything about that either. Your mother has always ribbed me about my sneaking through college and supports it by an inscription one of my teachers put into my annual:

> *He who burns the midnight oil will earn his way to fame,*
> *But he who sells the midnight oil will get there the same.*

Grandmother, at age eighty-one, had cataract surgery at the West Georgia Medical Center in LaGrange with general anesthesia and never was the same after that. Soon she was placed in the Florence Hand Nursing home. After a year or so there, she was discharged home to die. Grandmother had extensive rheumatoid arthritis and took eight to twelve aspirins a day. This in time damaged her kidneys and she ultimately passed away at home just feet away from where her husband had died twenty years earlier and in a bed next to my mother's. My mother visited her in the nursing home daily and took care of her while she was dying in our home. In many ways, my mother's care for her mother during this time paid my grandmother back for all she had done for her. Life is funny that way. What goes around comes around and we don't know God's plan. I have always been grateful that mother had the opportunity to be "the good daughter" as I feel it helped pay a debt that only she knew the emotional consequence of which and how much of a debt was owed.

I made a "B+" on my report. My first son goes by Clay and my daughter by Bess. I cannot express what a gracious savoir my grandmother was to me and not a day goes by that I don't think of her or something, uncharacteristic of whom you thought she was, she did to help me.

Jennie Cooper

M y mother's father was a pharmacist in LaGrange, Georgia, during and after the depression. At that time, there were very few physicians in Troup County and as a result, my grandfather was close friends with all of them. Having been a football player at the University of Georgia and a good golfer, he interacted with the doctors socially. His pre-depression home was next door to one of the first internists of LaGrange: Dr. Wallace Clark, and his daughter, Georgia, was one of my mother's best friends. During lunch many times his doctor friends would come to his pharmacy's "fount" to have lunch and talk. It was through this association that my mother developed a love and respect of the medical profession.

My mother grew up Presbyterian but married a Catholic, hence the nine miscarriages and the five male children she ended up with. She loved all of her pediatricians and gynecologists although she would admiringly refer to all of them as "my baby doctors." Up until about the third grade, my mother told me I was going to be "her priest" but she then decided I was going to be "her doctor." From that point on, she spoke to me not in tones of if but when I became a doctor. I fully bought into this. I must be funny that way; taking things literally. When my younger brother Jeff was born two days after my birthday on April 17th she called home from the hospital to speak to all of the children and announce the happy arrival. I was six at the time.

When it was my turn to talk to my mother, I skipped over the part about a baby and asked, "Why didn't I have a birthday party and what am I getting for my birthday this year?"

"John I am bringing home a little baby boy for your birthday."

I took this literally and ever since that day, I have considered Jeff to be mine and my relationship to him has been more like that of a father than of an older brother.

So by fourth grade, I knew I was going to be a doctor. My mother said things to me in which I could visualize the feeling of being a doctor. "They are the cat's meow John. I loved my doctors. Now when you are a doctor, be sure to get outside and have hobbies that keep you tanned. Nothing I hate more than seeing a pale limp wristed doctor walking through the hospital looking like he's not slept or been outside in years. They make a lot of money too John." My mother seeing the fruition of my becoming a doctor was so strong and believable that it made it easy for me to see it.

As I approached finishing high school, it dawned on me that the only way I could assure being successful was to be a doctor. I did not have the confidence or connections to be an assured success in business. My thinking in regards to being a doctor was that the hard part would be getting into medical school. If I could do that, then the skids would be greased to becoming a doctor and an opportunity to earn the benefits that entailed: helping others and assuring social standing and income.

I had never read anything nor had I been told anything about the power of visualization, although I practiced it daily. I visualized how happy my mother would be if I were a doctor. I visualized getting into medical school, getting my medical school diploma, and most importantly, I visualized signing my name with the M.D. after it. This was one of my most powerful things to visualize, signing a check with the M.D. on it and not saying anything, but with pride handing it to someone. The most powerful "success vision" I had by far was knowing how it would make my mother feel. She had been through so much and had undergone the silent ridicule of many as a result of her situation. I felt it would give her some degree of respect and standing. One of her son's had "made a doctor." I honestly believe that my becoming a doctor was more important for my mother than it was for me. My love of her and my spiteful memory of my father drove me daily. Somehow I felt my becoming a doctor and what it meant to mother would help make up for all she went through during the divorce. I felt that when and if Butch found out about me being a doctor, it would be more about a statement attesting to the success of mother as a parent; that she was not unfit.

When I got the letter of acceptance into medical school, I called my mother. At that time she was a teacher at Hogansville High School teaching Special Education. Someone in the school's office went and got her out of her room for the call. It was very difficult to get the statement out without crying, "Mother...I got in!"

After hanging up, I then visualized her telling everyone in the school's office and then all of her friends in LaGrange. The vision and its completion had come full circle and it felt good. I used the memory of how it felt to have been accepted to medical school to push me towards how it would feel to complete medical school. In other words utilizing the visualization technique and then achieving the goal builds on itself for the next accomplishment.

In mother's 1938 high school annual, two quotes were used to describe her, "As calm as a hurricane" and in being given the Hall of Fame award, "Jennie C. Davis-the ability to do as she pleases." She was indeed perfectly flawed and we adored her.

John C. McHugh M.D.

The Infamous Mother's Day Plane Trip

S everal years ago I had the idea that it would be special to visit my mother on Mother's Day by plane. I had a friend who was an ophthalmologist, a pilot and owned a single engine plane. I asked him if he would fly me down to LaGrange, Georgia, pick mother up, fly back to Gainesville to spend the day and then fly her back. In retrospect the itinerary for that day, was a bit much. My mother was about 75 at the time. I really don't know what I was thinking. Anyway, both my friend and my mother agreed to the plan and one Saturday morning I met Steve at the Gainesville airport to embark on the little adventure. It was a cloudy and overcast day. I did not appreciate the significance of that at the time, but anyone who knows anything about single engine planes is that you don't fly on overcast days. The reason is that if something happens to your "single engine" by the time you descend out of the clouds, there is no time to then find a place for an emergency landing. Unbeknownst to me, Steve had been recently rated to fly using instruments only, i.e. instrument rated. He was looking forward to utilizing his new skills and quietly excited about the prospect of flying by instruments for the trip. (John Kennedy Jr. was instrument rated...just saying.)

I had been in a small plane before. I flew around Augusta one time with another friend and I had been in them on fishing trips out west, so I was no stranger to this type of plane. The cockpit was very small and of course once the plane is running it is very loud. Steve gave me a set of headphones which allowed us to communicate and also served as noise reducers. The sky when we arrived at the airport, by my appraisal, was scattered clouds. Once we became airborne it was much less scattered. In fact, all I could see was white. It was as if we were a tiny capsule and then wrapped up in a sheet; nothing but white, tight quarters and noise. A sightseeing trip this was not to be.

Steve then told me about the flight plan. "We're flying over Atlanta's Hartsville Airport."

I jokingly asked, "The busiest airport in the world?"

"We're okay, I have a flight plan. I won't be flying where the other planes will be."

I ask, "Wouldn't it be better if we could see?"

"John, I have a flight plan and I have my instruments. The airport controller will be directing me. We're good. Don't worry about it."

About two hours later, Steve told me we are about there and we began to descend to the LaGrange airport. There was still no visibility but I saw the altitude change on the instrument panel and I saw a diagram of a runway. As we came down out of the clouds, I saw what appeared to be airport type structures, but then Steve opened up the throttle and we went back up quickly and began to circle around. "I overshot the runway. I'll get it this time," he says.

Meanwhile, I later learned, my mother was in the terminal talking with the attendants there and witnessed the whole missed runway thing. Before they knew that the plane they just witnessed was the one my mother was waiting on someone said, "Who are those idiots. They shouldn't be flying today."

My mother said sarcastically, "That's my ride."

On the second pass, Steve landed the plane without a problem. He then pulled out a black eye patch and put it on. The significance of which had to do with Will Rogers and Wiley Post. Wiley Post set records for flying in the 1920's and wore an eye patch that distinguished him. He and Rogers loved to fly together and, in fact, both were killed in a plane crash in Alaska. My mother came out to the plane to greet us and said, "They are laughing at you two. Did you overrun the runway?"

I said, "Put this on mom. It's a Wiley Post eye patch." We took some pictures of mother with the eye patch in front of the plane. She then said she wanted to think about the rest of the trip over lunch.

One of the things I loved about visiting my mother was going shopping and eating with her during my visit. We'd go to Walmart to get various things for her home, a Sinatra C.D. or two and then eat somewhere. She loved Ryan's buffet style menu because she could put things like cornbread and meat in a napkin and take it home. She always said as she slipped the food in her purse, "This for Cooper. He loves Ryan's cornbread."

On this visit mother did not want to go to Walmart, she wanted to buy a pair of shoes at Belk's. Having done that we then went to Ryan's for lunch. Steve and I were eating and mother was squirreling away treats for Cooper when this lady approached our table. In a tone very familiar to me and one I had heard many times growing up, "Well hello Jennie Cooper. How are you?" This tone was a "better than thou" tone and peculiar to LaGrange natives who knew mother before she left LaGrange. People who knew mother's circumstances commonly asked me, "John, is Jennie working?" The lady began to condescendingly inspect my mother's clothes, hair and the catfish tenders Mother was putting in a napkin.

"I am fine Mary Francis. How are you?"

"Just fine, just fine," she says. As if an afterthought she asked, "Who are these handsome young men with you?" Now she was inspecting Steve and me.

"These are two of my sons. They are both surgeons. They've flown down here on his plane, pointing to Steve, to visit me on Mother's Day. Wasn't that sweet of them? Have a nice day Mary Francis," she said as she completed packing her pocketbook buffet.

This was a classic mother retort and one I am sure she relished making. A sarcastic white lie delivered with a bite and a purpose. One thing about mother, she may not have had the best situation financially or a high position on the social hierarchy, but she never felt inferior to anyone. She'd reminded me of her favorite Eleanor Roosevelt quote many times, "No one makes you feel inferior without your help."

We drove back to the airport, parked and walked toward the plane.

"So mother, do you want to fly back to Gainesville with us?"

"John. There is no way in hell I'm getting into that plane. Not after what I saw."

"Well, I'll call you when we get back."

"I'm not holding my breath," she said sarcastically as she turned and went to her car.

Back in the plane, Steve said he had the option of a different flight plan for the trip home. "We'll go back by way of Athens this time." Again, nothing but white all around and all the way home.

We got back without a hitch and I called mother and told her she could breathe now and that all was well. I swore to myself I'd never fly in a single engine plane unless there were clear skies. The next day I did a procedure on a retired airline pilot. I mentioned to him my experience and he looked at me incredulously. "You went flying in a single engine plane with no visibility? That's stupid. I'll fly a 747 in a thunderstorm, but I wouldn't be caught dead in a single engine plane with clouds around."

Mothers do know best!

Rushton

M y brother Rushton was a beautiful person. Everyone who ever knew him will tell you the same thing. I never heard him ever say anything negative about someone. I did hear him very cleverly size up a person in few choice words and one would have to determine for themselves if it was negative or not. He got that trait from my mother. My mother adored Rushton; she adored all of her children, but really loved Rushton. When I had gotten settled as a urologist after residency and was in the black financially, I asked my mother if she could have anything in the world what would it be? She promptly said, "I want to visit Rushton with my family."

Rushton was the oldest of the five boys and he was always kind to me. In Columbus, Georgia, the yards behind the houses across the street, Flint Drive, were unfenced and where we played tackle football. The area was large and perfect for playing football except it had a slope of about thirty degrees. This slope soon became part of the strategy of each team depending which way you were facing. My brother Cooper always paired up with Bob and I was always with Rushton. I was in fourth grade at the time and Rushton would have been in high school and we perfected the down and out pass. The older brothers were always the quarterbacks and Bob and I the receivers.

I mention the above to make the point that Rushton and I were very much alike and I'd go so far as to say kindred spirits. Rushton found a guitar on the side of the road in someone's trash and learned to play it. No sooner had he learned a barre chord that he began to teach me. By fourth grade, I could play most every chord, including the barre chord, with ease.

We loved the Beatles and after seeing their debut on the now famous *Ed Sullivan Show* American debut we'd buy every album as they came out. The Beatles were a very large part of my childhood and I can match almost every period of my life to the release of one of their albums. When we lived in Columbus, it was the early Beatles, in Smyrna the middle Beatles with *Rubber Soul*, *Sgt. Peppers* and *The White Album* and then in LaGrange, *Abbey Road* and *Let It Be*.

In sixth grade I had a band and Rushton taught my friends and me how to play together and encouraged us to play at birthday parties. Our main song was "Gloria" written by Van Morrison and performed by The Shadows of Knight. To this day, when I pick up a guitar, I warm up with the familiar "E" "D" and "Am." He taught me to love music and every album he brought home I listened to over and over again, including all of the Beatle albums. I am to this day an avid Beatle fan and the first major purchase I made as a urologist was a box set of every Beatle CD for my brother Bob and me.

After the divorce, I had been relegated to live with my father; I moved into the house that had been converted into a business then back into a house. My father had a business involving selling magnetic signs for cars which he could customize. In the basement of the building, he spray-painted these signs and as a result, the house smelled like paint and he always had some vestige of the most recent project on his hands and face. The place was on the Atlanta Highway south of Smyrna, apart from any other residential home; so, Jeff and I were isolated from people our age, except for school. He went to an elementary school nearby, Fitzhugh Lee School, and I took a school bus to Nash Junior High, which was about five miles away. In the summer, I had a Greyhound bus ticket book I used to get to football practice. The bus stopped at a shopping center about a mile from Nash and I'd walk from there to the school then repeat the process in reverse after practice. Bob had moved to live with mother in LaGrange, Cooper lived with us while he finished high school, and Rushton lived with his girlfriend and worked at Lockheed Martin in Marietta. He had to take a test determining if he could place rivets in a certain location and at an acceptable speed. He couldn't, but he asked the guy next to him to do it for him, which he did, and Rushton got the job. He made about eighteen dollars an hour and for us at that time was very large amount of money and we were all very proud of him.

At the time of the divorce and move, I was in seventh grade and had to my name three albums, a The Who album where Peter Townsend was in a tub of baked beans, *Axis Bold as Love* by Jimi Hendrix and an older Beatles album. All of the albums we had except these three must have gone to LaGrange with Bob. I was very much aware of all of Hendrix's music, in particular songs from *Are You Experienced?* One day Rushton stopped by the "kennel," we called the house the kennel because at one time it had housed animals, to tell me he had gotten tickets to see Jimi Hendrix. Rushton, his girlfriend, and I went to the Atlanta Municipal Auditorium to see the show. One cannot imagine what a thrill it was to go to a concert and in particular this one. I think this act of kindness and awareness on Rushton's part speaks volumes. I knew every song and of course after the last song ended, Jimi destroyed a guitar on the amplifiers. Needless to say, there were not many other seventh graders with thick glasses in the audience.

With the money Rushton was making, he bought a 1967 Camaro with a 329 engine and four on the floor. It had in it something completely new: an eight track tape player. And of course, the first two eight track tapes he bought were the Beatles' *Sgt. Peppers* and *The White Album*. He dropped by the kennel and asked me to come out to the car and we listened to both in their entirety. Up until this time, the only thing you could listen to in a car was a radio, so this was a huge transition to be able to control not only the band you

listened to, but the song as well. For a nineteen year old
brother to sense my remorse of living without my mother and
my isolation I feel speaks volumes about the kind heart of my
brother Rushton.

When Cooper finished high school, he and Rushton
moved to LaGrange. They then began attending a junior
college just over the Georgia Alabama line in Wadley,
Alabama. A year or so later, Butch decided to move to Alaska
and as Jeff and I were no longer a part of his "schemes"; we
too moved to LaGrange. My poor little grandmother; now
there were six additional people living in her two bedroom
one bath home. Ten years of living alone and now her
daughter and five boys descended upon her, ravaging her
home and pocketbook. During this time, the Camaro was
taking a beating. At Southern Union Junior College, Rushton
started a band called The Fish Camp Band and began living
the life of a full-fledged hippie. Rushton was always a hippie
at heart, replete with the long hair, bell bottoms, smoking,
and doing all the stuff hippies do. Cooper and Rushton both
finished the junior college and both by an act of God and my
mother's help got into the University of Georgia. Keep in
mind there was no money forthcoming from my mother. All
of this was done by loans and grants conjured up by my
mother. She had a credit card that was used to its limits in a
few months and then for years she paid only the interest. As
unwise as this was financially, it served the purpose of
getting her two oldest boys started in Athens. In Athens,
Rushton continued his hippie ways and soon was back home;
Cooper finished a few years later with a degree in Physical
Education.

Soon after moving back to LaGrange, Rushton
married a smart and beautiful girl Shelia who my mother
loved. They rented a home and Rushton went to work selling
insurance. This lasted about two years or so and it became
clear that the domestic life was not Rushton's cup of tea. He
and Shelia divorced and Rushton and a few friends decided
to move to Panama City and have a go at making a living
playing music with remnants of The Fish Camp Band. This is
where Rushton's kindness again shows itself. Rushton chose
to go to Florida with a friend in his friend's car so he gave the

Camaro to me. I had just turned sixteen about this time and now was the proud owner of a rode hard and put up wet 1967 Camaro. The car was destroyed on the inside but the outside still looked good as there had been no major damage to the body. Rushton was like that, money or material things meant nothing to him. His giving me that car just as I needed one is the epitome of our relationship and how he always related to me.

I worked at NAPA auto parts throughout high school and bought stuff from the store to improve the Camaro. I used my earnings to have it painted and bought some lime green plush carpet from a friend for five dollars and replaced the old and mildewed carpet. I had the car a year before I figured out why the car always smelled like mildew. It was a leak that came in from the antenna. Finding this was huge because now the car didn't smell and the passenger side carpet didn't get soaked with every rain. I replaced everything from the water pump and back axel to the muffler and tail pipe, all NAPA parts. There was one thing about the car I could not fix and that was the clutch. On two occasions I saved up the money to have all the components of the clutch replaced, but each time it failed to correct the most frustrating thing about this car...a loud and jerky transition to move forward in first gear. I never could fix it and to this day, I remember dreading being parked on an uphill incline and having to start off in front of people. Years later I was recounting this attribute about the Camaro to a Chevrolet mechanic and he quickly said, "You can't use rebuilt parts for that. It has to be factory." NAPA parts like the clutch pad, pressure plates, and brakes are rebuilt. Damn it! I found in the box I have alluded to, a tax receipt for the Camaro and I have a patient who has a friend who is a sheriff and he said he may be able to find the Camaro today. If so, I plan to attempt to find and purchase it. It was the car I drove to college and the car for my first date with Karen, and yes her dorm was on an incline and I had to apologize in advance about being ready for a loud and jerky, bumpy take off.

Rushton initially struggled in Florida being in several bands and situations. The owners of bars would plead with him to play Jimmy Buffett songs, songs that the patrons knew and could sing along with. Time after time he'd be fired for not playing Buffett. He wanted to play his original music. After a second divorce, Rushton moved from Panama City to Orange Beach, Alabama, and began playing at the Flora-Bama. At that time, the owners of the Flora-Bama owned property across the highway from the Flora-Bama on the bay that had numerous small campers on it. Singer-songwriters such as Rushton could stay in these campers as payment for playing music. This is where Rushton was staying the first time we visited as an entire family. We rented a big house with a pool on the beach and Rushton would stop by and visit. Mother always asked him to play "Georgia" for her in the style of Ray Charles and they would sing it together. Oh how she loved the South and anything Georgia, "American by birth-Southern by the grace of God." She was never happier than when we could be at the beach as a family and that Rushton could be there. When we'd see him, it was obvious he was living the life of a down and out musician with all of the habits and life style which that entailed.

Rushton's original music developed as time went on and after a few years at the Flora-Bama, he became a regular musician there. Combining his lovable personality with songs that were funny yet clever, he established a following not only locally but with the people who vacationed in the Orange Beach area. Each week a new set of followers came to see his shows so that he came to know people from previous years. This built upon itself and in time every week his shows were filled with new listeners as well as ones who were returning vacationers. Our family went to Orange Beach the first week in August every year and we too became part of "the first week of August" group to go to the Bama and watch "Rusty." It was something to see and we were very proud of what Rushton had accomplished. There were two types of listeners at his performances. First there was the group that knew his songs and sang along, and then the newcomers who would be listening and when they heard the punch line of a song they broke out laughing and then they too were hooked on Rushton's music.

Rushton performed at the Flora-Bama for about eighteen years. During that time he married Millie Smedley and for the first time, probably in his lifetime, he was very content. He and Millie were soul mates and his music was continually being refined and improved. He had a large following for his shows and he enjoyed performing, writing music, and continuing his musical projects.

One day I received a phone call from Rushton. "Well John, you were right. I got the sh*t."

"What do you mean "You got the sh*t?"

"I have cancer. It's in my throat. I am going to have it removed next week." Listening to him I noted his voice was raspy. In fact, I had noticed his voice seemed very different on his latest CD, "We All Love a Woman with a Big Ole Ass." I remember commenting on this to my wife while we were listening to it on one occasion on the way home from Orange Beach.

What he had was a base of tongue cancer common in people who have smoked. When I asked a friend, who was an oncologist, what the prognosis of this type of cancers was, he just shook his head and said, "John that's a tough cancer and the treatment of it is rough. I am so sorry." Rushton had the tumor removed and the lymph nodes in his neck resected. He then had chemotherapy and radiation therapy. My brother Bob and I visited him on one occasion and on another I went down with my little brother Jeff. Rushton had lost a lot of weight and his face was disfigured by the surgery but he could talk in an understandable whisper by holding his hand over the tracheostomy. He spent much his day entertaining well-wishers and watching old cowboy movies and westerns. For some reason that was all he wanted to watch and he did it without any sound. In the room where his T.V. was located, all of the air vents had been closed off with masking tape. When I asked him why all the vents were amended in this way, he told me that the movement of air stimulated a very painful sensation in his ears. He played for us recordings of two songs he was working on and discussed them with such joy after we listened to them. One was called "Lost Dog" and the other "The B*tch Burned My Boat." We were now the Flora-Bama audience and hearing the new songs and clever lyrics for the first time responded just as the crowd would have. Oh how he loved sharing his music and popping the hook of the song and seeing the reaction.

One of the visitors was a singer-songwriter he knew and who had come by with his guitar to sing something he had written for Rushton. It all seemed nice enough at the first but the song morphed into a ballad about dying and meeting Jesus. Whereas the songs Rushton had just shared with us were funny, clever and easy to listen to, this guy's song was boring, uninventive, and at the time I felt was insensitive. Rushton listened to the whole thing nodding in approval paying one hundred percent attention. After the song and small talk Rushton thanked the guy for stopping by and he left.

Knowing that Rushton was not known to be a religious person I asked him, "How did you sit through that with such patience and attentiveness?"

In a voice becoming more weakened as the day progressed, I barely made out the response. "John, he did not mean any harm. He is a recovering alcoholic Christian...the worst kind."

The next day Rushton asked me to drive him to a music store where his favorite guitar was being repaired. Jeff had given Rushton the gift of having it repaired several months previously. After picking up the guitar we then went to the hospital for an additional chemotherapy treatment. We were in a 1973 Buick as I remember and Rushton was very proud of it and loved that it was so big. He told me to stop at the entrance of the oncology clinic at the hospital and he went in while I parked the car. After walking a few yards he came back to the car and pointing at the guitar he said twice, "John, lock it tight!" When I parked I put the guitar in the trunk very carefully and then made sure all the doors were locked. I checked them all twice and also pulled up on the trunk to be sure it was engaged.

As I walked into the hospital I was struck by the optimism and spirit of my brother. He had to know that when you have positive lymph nodes, you've had chemotherapy and radiation after radical surgery, that your prognosis is not good. In addition to this, the cancer itself had taken from him the very part of his body necessary to do what he loved the most, to sing. I saw none of this in him, absolutely no pessimism or lack of joy for the present or future. Inside I met his doctor and then I sat with Rushton while the chemotherapy was given through a port under his clavicle. As the medicine coursed through the tubing into my brother, we talked.

"You know John, ever since I was in high school, there was always something tapping on my shoulder, a desire for something that I did not have. Beer and smoking cigarettes helped. I have always had a real life monkey on my back. Valium helps but the best is pot." "Pot calms me," he said while he began tapping his right shoulder with the fingers of his right hand. I remembered all the times I had watched Rushton perform at the Flora-Bama and during breaks he'd walk across the street to the campers and find friends sitting on makeshift porches in front of the bay and smoke marijuana. He'd always ask me if I cared to partake, but I never did. I did try pot in college but I did not like smoking. Once on a Thanksgiving visit to LaGrange, I told Rushton that he should not be smoking. I mentioned the association of smoking and lung cancer, but I also made the point that it causes lung disease that may make it difficult to breathe as he got older. Surprisingly Rushton's response had a bit of a bite to it, "John I smoke because I like it. You don't smoke because you don't like it. You are not any better than me or anyone else for not doing something you don't like." I think this is where he came up with the line, "John you were right. I got the sh*t" came from.

The comments about the monkey on his back must have been Rushton's trying to justify why he smoked and why, even though he was dying from smoking, he felt it was a necessary habit for him. I said nothing but the thought did begin me thinking about his dying. I saw the whole process in my mind's eye and it didn't help that as a physician I had witnessed many people succumb to cancer. It was not going to be pretty. I held back tears. To this day I do not know where what I said next after reflection of his anticipated death came from or why I would have said it.

"Rushton, do you worry about God and not having been religious? I mean what happens when a person dies?"

"Yeah, I think about it. But you know John, God isn't stupid. What am I supposed to do? Pray and ask forgiveness, or to be cured, or to go to heaven? He knows who I am, who I've been and I won't be able to pull no sh*t on him."

Without any prompting from me he continued, "Don't worry about me John, I'm happy. If you had told me twenty years ago that I would achieve what I have done with my music I would have laughed at you. I am a satisfied man. I have accomplished the things that I wanted to accomplish. Don't worry about me, I'm good."

I cannot tell you how comforted I was by what he said to me then and now as I write this. A part of my fear in dying is that I will not have accomplished all that I hoped to do. Rushton was in a good place and that gave me peace. He was at peace with his situation. He probably knew that saying he was content would also give peace to the ones who loved him.

Rushton and his wife Millie loved Jamaica and had been there many times. Rushton enjoyed going inland and experiencing that which most tourists never see. When he was getting over the treatments, I asked him if there was anything he wished he could do or want, and he said he wanted to go to Jamaica again. My wife and I purchased a trip to an all-inclusive resort and first class plane tickets. When I was visiting him, the trip was all he talked about and how much he was looking forward to it. Millie as well on many occasions spoke of how the anticipation of the trip in many ways was therapeutic for Rushton. The trip kept his spirits up. As the time for departure neared Rushton began to deteriorate but despite this, he and Millie wanted to make the trip. Once in flight, we are not sure if it was an altitude issue, Rushton had a seizure and was essentially comatose for the entire trip. In Jamaica, he was taken by wheelchair to the van which was to take them to the resort and once there Rushton spent the next two days in bed. Millie decided that it would be best to go home and the reverse sequence of events ensued until he was back in Florida. He died the next day.

Months later there was a Rusty McHugh memorial event at the Flora-Bama and I was telling Millie it was a shame about the trip and how I was sorry she went through so much trouble and effort. I commented that Rushton may not have known he even went.

"Oh John you don't understand. He loved Jamaica and his last memory on earth was of something he loved. It was perfect, it was a gift, it was just how he would have wanted it."

Rushton was cremated and small urns of Rushton were given to all of his close friends and family. Millie emptied the remaining ashes at the base of a waterfall during a small ceremony in Jamaica a year after his death.

On a lighter note: Thanksgiving was the one holiday that Rushton seldom missed coming home and as it turned out, it was a Thanksgiving that Karen accompanied me to meet my family after we were engaged. As previously stated, I adored my grandmother and was in hopes that I could have grandmother's wedding ring for my wedding. I saw it as a huge compliment and asked my mother about it. She felt it was also a compliment and that she'd speak to my grandmother in advance of me broaching the issue. Apparently it was a bit of an issue to my grandmother. Mother said that she had to "reason" with my grandmother and she agreed to let me have it. The ring was petite with a small diamond and the significance of it having been given to her by Robert Cooper Davis during the depression was overwhelming to me. As I viewed it, that my wife could wear it would be a perpetual honor to the two of them. So I am out in front of our house talking with Rushton and he said, "John do you love this girl?"

Surprised I said, "Yes Rushton I do. Why?"

"Well you better love her if she is going to wear grandmother's ring."

Rushton was right, God isn't stupid and that is precisely why Rushton is indeed in heaven.

Carol

M y mother and father got divorced when I was in seventh grade. I say divorced...my father got rid of my mother and she moved to LaGrange from Smyrna, Georgia, with five boys, not a penny to her name and no job, to live with her mother. The home was purchased by my grandfather in 1930, was a block off the downtown square and across the street from the 1st Presbyterian Church. The house is where my mother grew up and the church she attended with her parents and sister. When we showed up, my grandmother Bessie Clay Morgan Davis was seventy-three, a widow of ten years and living off social security. The house was depression era architecture, two stories, two bedrooms, a bathroom without a shower, and a "television room" upstairs. Downstairs there was an enclosed porch, a kitchen, a dining room and the living room. There was a window air conditioning unit in the television room and it was in this room where I slept on a cot that was kept during the day folded in a hallway closet. In the summer we depended on the attic fan to draw the never cool night air across our bodies. Given that I had been forced to live with my father by the courts, living in LaGrange in this home was wonderful. I did however have very ill feelings toward my father who was now in Alaska with a new wife and child. No money was ever to be forthcoming from him. He was history to me both physically and emotionally.

I moved to LaGrange with about six weeks left in eighth grade and started ninth grade at LaGrange High School the next fall. In my home room there was a girl who sat in front of me whose family was very prominent in town. Over the course of the next several weeks, we spoke from time to time before the teacher took roll but little more than that. For some reason it always happened to me that people would ask, "What does your dad do?" I hated it. I didn't have the courage to say that, "Well, my father and mother are divorced and he lives in Alaska and I live with my grandmother." So I'd say what I felt was a respectable answer, "He is in real estate." My self-esteem was at a low point due to all of the changes but accentuated by the fact that I wore glasses. When I say glasses, I am talking about the kind that resemble the bottom of a coca-cola bottle. I had gotten a new pair of glasses twice a year since fourth grade. To this day my eyes water when I think about seeing the accounting of my glasses at the ophthalmologist, thirty or so entries of my mother having paid five dollars a week on a several hundred dollar bill. So that Carol even took the time to speak to me each morning in home room was remarkable to me. She introduced me to her friends, she made a point to say hello in the hall during class changes, and treated me as a friend.

One day in home room, she turned around in her desk and out of nowhere said, "John you are a good person, you are funny and you are smart." It is though she sensed the baggage I was carrying and that it was weighing me down. Probably she noticed the low self-esteem body language in me, mannerisms like not making eye contact.

To this day, I have no clue from whence that remark or observation came from or how she possessed the insight to see through me. From that point on throughout high school, college and to this day, she has been one of my biggest advocates. It may sound trite, but she believed in me before I believed in myself. Outside of my mother and grandmother, I feel in my heart that Carol made me feel special and that was exactly what I needed at that very point in my life. I was recently looking for a picture of a friend in my high school annual and happened upon Carol's year end note. Although I didn't remember it and had not read it probably since high school, it was very characteristic. Full of encouragement, full of complimenting me on my achievements, telling me I had potential to achieve anything I planned to pursue and congratulating me on being one of the graduation speakers.

    To the graduate who might be reading this one day, you too not only have potential but you have someone you may not be aware of who is quietly encouraging you and serving as your "Carol." Acknowledge it and don't let that person...or yourself down.

Mr. Fulford

I   t was in eighth grade at Nash Junior High that I first
    enjoyed a class as being practical. It was early in the school
    year and it had just been mandated by the court that I live
with my father. Later that year my father allowed my younger
brother and me to live with my mother and I completed the last
six weeks of my eighth grade at Hill Street School in LaGrange.
It was the year of the presidential election between Hubert
Humphries and Richard Nixon. I remember having assignments
which required me to get information about the candidates and
write a report. During one of my once a month weekend
visitation with my mother, I went to the two campaign head
quarters on the square in LaGrange. I was given at no cost to me
stickers, pins, and informative brochures about the two
candidates. It was the first time I enjoyed anything related to
school courses. I have been a student of history and politics ever
since.

The second time I was ever enthralled with a class was
in ninth grade Economics taught by Mr. Fulford. I was
fascinated by the history of Adam Smith, the stock market, and
Mr. Fulford's commentary on the election coverage. Each
student was able to buy a pretend stock and then follow its
progress. I chose Bethlehem Steel. By doing this we learned
about the market's gyrations, how money could be made or lost,
and dividends. I also first learned of the politicalization of the

news. In one class he expressed frustration at the way a particular network handled their interpretation of a speech by one of the candidates.

"I just wish they would not tell us what to think or what they think the speech was about or what the candidate was saying. I can do that myself without their help!"

Up until that moment I just assumed that if they said it on television, it was true and not an interpretation. The idea that what and how someone reported the news could be done in such a way to promote a particular political view was foreign to me.

I liked Mr. Fulford very much. He appeared to me a very smart and sensible man who also was very businesslike and strict. While I was a student at LaGrange High, he was promoted to assistant principal. He spoke to me most every day of my high school career as he stood at an area in the morning just outside of the principal's office where the students enter and often times at the same spot during class changes. Another thing about Mr. Fulford that I noted was that he purchased a home in a very nice neighborhood in LaGrange. I knew this because I occasionally rode around with my grandmother, mother, my grandmother's sister and her daughter on Sunday afternoons. (Since I did not drink and had zero social life outside of school, this represented the extent of my social life.) We'd start by going through the cemetery and look at my grandfather's grave or any recent addition and then stop at the Dairy Queen for a fudge dipped cone. Then we'd cruise the nice neighborhoods and the women would discuss any interesting gossip related to homes. In other words, the homes and who lived in them determined the conversation. It was during one of these rides that I learned that Mr. Fulford had purchased one of the nice homes. I remember being proud of him and that he probably made the money in the stock market because he taught economics. It made me like him even more. I did not begrudge his success; I emulated it.

When I was a senior, I was sent to the principal's office by a substitute teacher because of talking, a common behaviorial issue of mine, and a trait commented about on every report card in high school. "Disrupting others" by excessive talking is how the teachers would phrase it. I went down to the principal's office and Mr. Fulford was there just inside the door talking to a secretary.

"What brings you this way John?" he said.

"The substitute teacher for Mrs. Beckham sent me down here for talking," I said.

"Go into my office John, I'll be in there in a minute," he said with little emotion and looking at me over his glasses. In a couple of minutes he came in and sat at his desk and said, "John, have a seat on the couch there. How are you doing?"

"I am fine Mr. Fulford."

"Listen I have got to go to a meeting. You sit there for about ten minutes and then go back to class. Look dejected when you go back in the room...and be quiet." And with that, Mr. Fulford got up and left the office. I found something interesting to read for about ten minutes and then went back to class.

To this day I have always been fascinated by people in positions of responsibility or power who know how to use it. Mr. Fulford was that way. I currently have friends who are lawyers, judges, and politicians, and I know the ones that know how to ethically and appropriately use their influence, and the ones that have no clue. If one does not know the nuances of exerting the level of power of a certain position, then one will always exert all the power and as a result, use power when it is not necessary. On the other hand, there are those with power who are afraid to use it because they fail to understand what the acceptable application of it is and what is not. I remember acknowledging how he had handled my situation and saying to myself, "Boy that was cool." He handled my talking misdemeanor exactly with just the right touch. He knew that for me what he did was all that was necessary. It reminds me of one time my grandfather caught my mother smoking in their home's bathroom. As my mother was coming out of the bathroom with cigarette smoke trailing her, he said, "Jennie, those cancer sticks are going to kill you." He then just kept on walking and that was all that was said.

LaGrange was blessed to have the Callaway Foundation. The Callaway Foundation gave money for everything and also ran a complex that included an Olympic size swimming pool, a gym replete with a ping pong room, weights, and a large auditorium. This auditorium is where I gave my high school speech and where four years previous I was caught with my friend drinking beer. It was in the Callaway Foundation Library that I studied for the MCAT as a junior in college. Another thing the Callaway Foundation did was give a scholarship each year to ten deserving students from the three high schools in Troup County. It was a big deal in general and particularly to my mother and grandmother. They sat on our front porch every afternoon reading the LaGrange paper and well knew that not only was the money important, they also knew that the ten recipient's pictures and biographies would be on the front page. My mother on many occasions mentioned how important it would be to receive this scholarship. All the people that had received it in the past were always very smart and were going to schools I'd never heard of, like Furman.

So the paper came out one day in the spring of my graduation and sure enough, yours truly was on the front page of the paper with a bunch of very smart and deserving students. This represented the first true notable achievement in my life and was my mother ever happy. It makes me happy to this day to remember how proud she and my grandmother were. Every relative in Troup County, and there were many, cut out the pictures and the article and brought it by to my mother and congratulated her. Cutting an article out of the paper about a person and then either mailing it with a note or dropping it by the person's house is a very Southern thing.

The next day as I am entering the school, Mr. Fulford is standing just outside the office in his customary location. "John, you got a minute?"

"Yes, sir," I said concerned that some teacher had filed a complaint about me. Earlier that week I had sneaked out the back of English class about five minutes before lunch without the teacher noticing and no sooner had I left that the principal's office came over the intercom asking was I in the room. Then the teacher noticed I wasn't and then I heard all about it from my classmates when they arrived at the lunch room.

We went into his office, he shuts the door, motioned for me to sit on the couch, and he sat at his desk. Mr. Fulford as I remember had a Richard Nixon type four o-clock shadow and he had the habit of leaning his head forward and cupping his chin in one of his hands and speaking while peering over his black rimmed glasses. This gave the impression that he was thinking and considering his words carefully. So we sat for a minute or so with him thinking and rocking back and forth massaging his chin and looking into the distance.

"John, congratulations on winning the Hatton Lovejoy scholarship, you deserve it."

"Thank you sir."

"You know John, they normally give that scholarship based on academic achievement. I am sure you are aware that your grades and SAT scores are not upper tier. In other words, you received that scholarship because of who you are, your involvement in school activities, your family situation, your involvement in sports, and that you've kept your nose clean. Several of the members of the committee went to bat for you to get this and I thought it was important to let you know that. I know you will not let us down. I am very happy for you and your family."

I asked Mr. Fulford many years later if he felt I had correctly remembered his role in my getting the scholarship. He said, "Let's just say I put in a good word for you."

86

The Key Club

I played football, baseball, and wrestled as a freshman at LaGrange High. Although baseball was my favorite sport, my eyesight had deteriorated to the point that my glasses made a baseball look the size of a golf ball. So after my freshman year I had given up on playing baseball. If you played sports, one of your classes was athletic study hall. I don't quite know what that was supposed to achieve as I don't ever remember having a teacher or anyone studying during that hour. I do remember meeting a fellow athlete who would become one of my best friends. I say one of my best friends; I was not one of his best friends. I was his best go to friend when his other friends were busy. I was okay with it; I liked him. He was bad, but clever bad, and I was drawn to that quality. I got to know him in the study hall playing a game where you'd flip a coin and call whether you thought the heads or tails would match. If you were right, you won the coin denomination of choice. Of course he would do his best to cheat or gain some unfair advantage, but again, I liked that in him. I also liked that he was the best baseball player for the school as a freshman. He was a left-handed pitcher, had a lot of older friends, each having older friend type habits in which he indulged, and I felt privileged when he included me.

One day during playing "match", he asked me if I wanted to go the Callaway Foundation dance the upcoming Friday. We weren't old enough to drive, so the plan was for me to walk to his house and from there to walk to the auditorium where the dance was to be held. The reason I had to go to his house was to allow his parents to verify that he was going to the dance

with me and not an older friend in a car and all that that
entailed. He was warned by his mother repeatedly about what
he was to do and not to do and what time he was to be home. I
thought it was a bit much and suggestive of a blighted past of
which I was not aware. It dawned on me as we walked away and
he took out a pack of cigarettes from inside his socks and lit one
up that I was being used as his "cover." I was a useful idiot so to
speak.

     As it turned out, the week before I was one of four
freshman students accepted to be in the LaGrange High Key
Club. To my mother and me, this was a big deal. The teacher
advisors and all of the current members had to nominate and
approve me as a member. It was in the paper, and as it concerned
me, I had never seen my mother so proud. I was very much aware
of what it meant to my mom to be without a husband or a job
and having to return to her home town for her mother to take
care of her. I was intimately aware that anything her children
did that was good was a positive reflection on my mother and I
was all about doing right by her. It was in this setting that my
friend and I set out for the dance. Since we had no car, we took
short cuts through the back of people's yards and through
woods that connected the various roads. We were cutting
through some woods near the auditorium when my friend told
me to follow him to a mound of rocks. As he began to remove the
rocks, the tops of beer bottles became visible. It was a Miller
Pony eight-pack.

     "Let's drink a few before we go in. How about it?" he
said.

     "I don't know about that. Let me think on that," I said.

     He pulled out a container used for pills but in it was a
long strip of Close-Up toothpaste. "Don't worry about it. We'll
gargle with this stuff and no one will ever know or suspect
anything."

     We drank four a piece and made our way down to the
dance. No sooner did we enter the auditorium, than I saw in
front of the door, a table of four mothers. I considered turning
around, but before I could, one of the mothers said to my friend,
"Have you been drinking?" We did not even have a chance. Based
on previous behavior of which I was unaware, the chaperones
already knew he'd been drinking and then by association me as

well. "Both of you come with me." Next thing I knew, I was in a small room with two of the mothers and a police officer. I could not believe what was happening and I was scared to death. Immediately I thought of how my mother would feel upon hearing of the news and then the Key Club retracting my membership flashed across my mind. As the questioning began in earnest, I noted that all of the questions were directed at my friend and when asked point blank whether he had been drinking he denied it effortlessly and with indignation. After several minutes of consultation with the officer, one of the mothers said, "Well we know you have been drinking. We are going to let you two in this time but if you ever try this again, we will put you under the jail. Is that clear?"

In unison and very contritely we said, "Yes, ma'am." And with that, they let us in.

Once inside, I was beside myself for what I had just experienced. What had I almost done? It scared the hell out of me. My friend, on the other hand, was now a celebrity and was going around the dance floor breathing on people saying, "No I haven't been drinking!" I don't think I told my mother what had happened, but I can tell you for weeks I was worried that a Key Club officer would be calling. They didn't.

For the remainder of high school, I never had another drop of alcohol. As often happens in life, one negative experience, if experienced at just the right time and one learns from it, can positively affect the course of one's life.

Coach Alise

C oach Alise was a football coach who agreed to be the wrestling coach. I think this used to be a common occurrence that the athletic department head hired football coaches and then used them as well for other sports. I am not sure Coach Alise had ever been a wrestling coach before. It didn't matter. He knew athletes and he could learn the wrestling part. He was a short, stocky and a no-nonsense person who was tough but fair. One time we were having wrestling practice and a basketball player walking through made a remark making fun of our ninety eight pound wrestler. He overheard it and made the guy, who was much larger than the wrestler, wrestle the small guy and of course the small guy easily pinned him in short order. That put an end to passer bys making remarks about us and illustrates the toughness of Coach Alise.

I wrestled in the one thirty-eight weight class although my normal weight was one fifty-five. Football season was the sport before the wrestling season so I tried to gain weight during the former and then immediately started dieting to lose weight for the latter. Unlike most students, I loved cafeteria food, particularly the milk and the fresh rolls. Each day at lunch during football season, I'd go around to the girls I knew that did not like milk and didn't eat their rolls and put them on my plate. It was the beginning of a lunch ritual for me. During wrestling season, as the days approached a tournament, I'd bring some low calorie dish from home and hardly eat anything. Unbeknownst to me, all of my activities were observed by Coach Alise. As well, although I did not view myself as poor, everyone knew my mother's situation, that I had four brothers and we all lived with my grandmother. I guess I gave the impression of being in need. Okay...we were in need and living off our Grandmother.

One day I was coming into the gym to get ready for wrestling practice and Coach Alise asked me if he could speak to me. He had a huge roll of meal tickets. At LaGrange High, students bought the meal tickets and then gave them to the cafeteria cashier when they got their lunch.

"John, here."

"What do you mean coach?"

"Take these."

"Why coach? I don't need them. Coach, I don't..."

"John," pushing the roll of several hundred meal tickets into my hands, "take them." He then turned and walked away.

I looked down at the roll noting how heavy they all were and quickly hid them between my books. Being very conscious that someone may have seen what had transpired, I quickly continued down to the wrestling area. I experienced a mixture of emotions. Was I viewed as poor by everybody? Why did he pick me to give the tickets? I was at once both embarrassed and yet very grateful.

Later I told my mother what had happened and she brushed it off and simply said, "John, don't look a gift horse in the mouth."

Coach Alise and I never spoke of it again...but I'll never forget his random act of kindness... in a Coach Alise kind of way.

Dr. Davis

O kay, my mother whom I adored told me she wanted me to be a doctor. One may think that this is backward thinking, however in my case it is not. My mother did indeed know what was best; she was smart that way. Since I can remember, I always liked reading about the military schools in the back of Southern Living. I can vividly see the ads with the cadets in their uniforms and the formidable buildings in the background. The thought of being a cadet somewhere and getting to do activities like obstacle courses was a very exciting and appealing thing to me. I have no clue why wanting to wear a uniform came from. Here's the thing, I did not want to be in the military per se...I did have a fear of being shot. Now, if I knew for sure that I could be in the real military, have all the experience that that entailed, and return in one piece alive, I would have happily signed up for that. I viewed being at a military school as setting me apart from the majority of students applying to medical school. No one told me this; it just made sense to me. I did not make overly good grades and my SAT was average at best. When 1200 was considered good, I made 1000. I took it a second time and made in the low 900's. I had good reason to feel that getting into medical school was a long shot. I had my goal, but I did not have the plan. That is where the military school angle came into play.

The father of the girl I dated in high school was a judge and knew political people and would have helped me get into one of the military academies. The problem was that my vision was so bad this was not a possibility. I would have loved to have gone to the Citadel, but it was a private school and out of state and I could not afford that. That left North Georgia College in Dahlonega, Georgia, and as it turned out, the school where my grandfather went in 1907 before going to the University of Georgia to play football. It is a state supported school and the tuition was essentially covered by the Hatton Lovejoy scholarship I received from The Callaway Foundation in LaGrange.

North Georgia had a good reputation for getting its pre-med students into medical school. One of the professors responsible for this was Dr. Tom Davis, chairman of the Chemistry Department. So based on this, I elected to major in chemistry and as a result, Dr. Davis was my advisor. In my first meeting with him, he recommended I take Chemistry 101, History 101, and math. I was in the highest math class in high school and he asked me if I wanted to start with Calculus. I asked him did I have to. He said that actually the pre- med curriculum requires a lot of chemistry and biology but that the math could be any class. Knowing that I needed to make as many "A"s as I could to get into medical school, I asked if I could take Math 101. He pointed out that it looked like I had taken that as a freshman in high school and was I sure I wanted to take such a low level math course. I said I was very sure I wanted an easy math class if that was all that was required. As it turned out, the level of math of the two classes I took were more like what I had taken in eighth grade. They were perfect.

Chemistry 101 was full of pre-med students. The professor, Mr. Woolfolk, asked everyone who was pre-med to raise their hand and all but two people in the class were pre-med. It seemed everyone in the class also had the new Texas Instruments calculator. I could not afford one so I bought a slide rule from the school book store for about three dollars. I had never used one, however, once I learned to use it, it worked like a charm. It was my calculator throughout my college career.

The first order of business in the chemistry class was to take a pre-chemistry placement test. I think the real purpose of this was to allow Dr. Davis to see who was and who was not promising material and to better advise a student who thought it was cool to be pre-med but did not have the aptitude for what it would require. A few days after I had taken the exam, I was summoned to see Dr. Davis in his small office just off the lecture hall.

"John I have your results of your chemistry placement test here." Shaking his head he continued, "Although the scores are not bad, they are far below what I'd expect for a serious pre-med student and the successful attainment of admission to a medical school. It may be that you should reconsider the doctor pathway. What other professions interest you?"

I didn't answer, I felt nauseated. All of my aspirations and those of my mother flew through my head and I could already feel what failure felt like.

"Can I still take the pre-med courses we have set up?"

"Sure John, I just wanted to make sure your expectations are realistic going forward."

"Thank you," I said, and I got up and left.

During my freshman year at North Georgia College, I made all "A"s and one "B." The "B" was because I had two finals on the same day and I wrongfully elected to study only for the chemistry final and not the physics final. I had an "A" in physics then made a "C" on the final giving me a "B." I was so upset that I wrote the professor pleading him to allow me to retake the test and explaining that I had "put all my eggs" in my chemistry basket. He was unmoved and I was livid. I am not saying I was right, I just didn't think it was fair to have had an "A" all quarter only to be ruined by the final.

In retrospect, did Dr. Davis see something in me that out shone the results of the placement test? Did he in fact tell me to consider another career path to really make me work harder to make pre-med work? I don't know, but knowing what I observed in him over the years since, he just may have been encouraging me. I graduated Cum Laude with one of the highest if not the highest GPA in my cadet class at North Georgia. Around twenty years after graduating from college, and as a urologist in Gainesville, Georgia, I diagnosed prostate cancer in Dr. Davis and performed the surgery to remove it. I was honored that he chose me for his surgeon.

Dr. Davis is as responsible as anyone for my successful journey to becoming a doctor and I will always be grateful to him.

Mr. Lail

H ave you ever stopped to consider how dry and boring organic chemistry is? I majored in chemistry and to this day don't understand a bit about it. The most prominent thing I remember about chemistry is how much I hated the chemistry labs. What was that about? You have to go to the one hour class and then twice a week you have a lab in the afternoon. If chemistry is your major, you are in the lab all year and particularly painful is the fall and spring. I distinctly remember burning copper on a Brunsen burner to see what color the flame was and looking out of the lab window over the North Georgia College drill field. My fraternity brothers knew I was a chemistry major and that I had labs in the afternoons, usually Tuesdays and Thursdays. One day on a beautiful spring afternoon, I was dejectedly looking out over all the students doing fun things on and about the luscious green drill field. Just beyond the drill field, I noted a couple playing tennis and, after taking a closer look, realized it was a fraternity brother of mine playing tennis with my girl friend. I then remembered he happened to confirm that morning with me the fact that I'd be in lab. We called that "snaking." Seeing this only added to my misery, although I did admire the guy's bravado.

In the fall of my sophomore year, I took a required English Literature class with Mr. Lail. I had never taken literature and the only two books I had ever read were a Jack

Dempsey biography and *In Cold Blood*. My mother adored both
Jack Dempsey and Truman Copote and as I adored my mother, I
read what she recommended. Mr. Lail was a tall man who
exuded both confidence and passion. This was new to me as I
had stereotyped anyone who would like literature as someone
other than a man's man. He did not fit the mold of the classic
professorial English teacher. Mr. Lail's persona reminded me
more of my coaches in high school than someone who would
love literature. It was striking to me and a teachable moment.

What Mr. Lail did for me was to open up the world of
English literature. It all started with Robert Herrick's poem *To
the Virgins, to Make Much of Time* published in 1648. The poem
espouses the concept of Carpe Diem or "seize the day."

> Gather ye rosebuds while ye may,
> Old Time is still a-flying;
> And this same flower that smiles today
> Tomorrow will be dying.
>
> The glorious lamp of heaven, the sun,
> The higher he's a-getting,
> The sooner will his race be run,
> And nearer he's to setting.
>
> That age is best which is the first,
> When youth and blood are warmer;
> But being spent, the worse, and worst
> Times still succeed the former.
>
> Then be not coy, but use your time,
> And while ye may, go marry;
> For having lost but once your prime,
> You may forever tarry.

I was overtaken by literature. I loved the romantics, I
took a quarter of Shakespeare and then another of Mr. Lail's
classes. He loved Tennyson and it was in Mr. Lail's class that I
learned that the line, "Tis better to have loved and lost than to
never have loved at all" was about a male friend who had passed

away. My quarterly Literature class became my favorite subject matter in school and I enjoyed studying for the tests.

One day after a class I followed Mr. Lail to his office and asked him, "Is it possible for me to minor in English Literature?" I wasn't sure if I'd have enough time to take the necessary courses.

"I don't see why not and in fact I'd encourage you to do just that. You might run it by Dr. Davis and see if he sees any issue with it."

"Mr. Lail is it possible to minor in English Literature without having to write a paper? I'd rather take courses that I can study for and take a test and not have to write something that requires research or do the footnotes stuff."

"John I think I can configure your minor without you having to write a paper if that's what you want."

"Well then, I am in. I'll speak to Dr. Davis and thank you so much for enlightening me with literature. It has been such a welcomed reprieve to all the sciences I have had to take."

Dr. Davis was fine with the plan and now at each advisor meeting he balanced the requirements for medical school and those to have a minor in English Literature. Well after college, I watched a movie starring Robin Williams called *Dead Poets Society* and in many ways the storyline is similar to what happened to me. Chemistry was a means to an end and Literature is what inspired me. Mr. Lail was my John Keating. I loved throwing in the various quotes I had learned studying Shakespeare in casual conversation with friends and explaining the context after observing their puzzled faces.

Things were going along swimmingly well, I had gotten into medical school, lettered in soccer, had a girlfriend, and then it happened. The last English course I had to take somehow slipped by the plan that Mr. Lail and I had constructed. The professor was the same one who taught the dreaded freshman English 101 course. She was strict but I liked her and the fear of not doing well made me a better student. What surprised me about English 101 was that it was not much different than math, there were rules and when you used and applied the rules then you did well in English. On the very first day of the last quarter of my college career, she told the class about the course and then she said, "And you will be required to write a paper on a writer from the era we will be studying."

I raised my hand, "Does that mean we have to do references and footnotes and stuff like that. I was told this class did not require a term paper."

"You were told wrong, you will be required to write a paper properly referenced and without plagiarism. I will be checking on each student's progress throughout the quarter so don't wait until the last minute to do the paper."

Well...I waited until the last minute, unknowingly plagiarised and she gave me an "F." This made my "A" average a "C" giving me the only "C" I made in college. This does not diminish the immense pleasure and benefit of what having minored in English Literature did for me.

Damn references and footnotes!

Studying Shakespeare in Gaillard Hall at North Georgia College: I bought the study lamp at Roses in LaGrange and my glasses are being held in place by tissue making the hinges fit tighter so I could read without them falling off.

Tony

My freshman year of college is a blur to me in many ways. I arrived at North Georgia College in the fall of 1973 in Rushton's worn out 67 Camaro listening on its eight track tape player to The Band. Since North Georgia is a military school, my first experience as a college student was a week of cadet orientation called "Frog week." This entailed a crash course in military orientation, being awoken at all times of the morning, inspections, exercise, and being hazed. Once school started, my daily routine involved a morning inspection, marching to the "chow hall" for breakfast, and then classes. In the evening, freshmen were required to be in their room by 7 p.m. for study hall, which included a fifteen minute break at 10 p.m. All of this was not really a big deal to me as I knew no other college life existence and I needed to study to make A's for medical school anyway. At the end of the first quarter, any freshman who had a 3.0 or better did not have to endure study hall but I continued it as if I had to. To me it was all about the grades as I had firmly affixed to my head that I had to get into medical school. The wishes of my mother and the disdain for my father drove me. I have often said that my father was the best negative positive influence in my life.

I have mentioned that almost every student in my freshman class who was a chemistry major was in the pre-med program. But as often happens when the reality of college life sets in and other interests prevail, fewer and fewer students become valid candidates. One such person in my class, whom I barely knew but had noticed, was Tony. I didn't like him. He was from Chickamauga, Georgia, confident, overtly cocky, athletic, and very smart; but, by the end of his freshman year, his grades did not reflect this. He had, as I remember, a 2.8 or so and definitely on paper not likely to be getting into medical school. A series of events delayed my getting to know Tony better and ultimately his becoming my best friend.

At North Georgia I was in the Mountain Order of Colombo, a mountaineering society. I had always wanted to rappel and climb mountains so the opportunity to join was a no brainer. We trained on a rappelling tower behind Sirmon's Hall while on campus and then on weekend outings on Mount Yonah. Mount Yonah is where the Rangers train so it was very exciting to be climbing and rappelling where they did. Behind our dorm was Crown Mountain and it was here during the first American gold rush in 1829 that some of the mining companies blasted and tunnelled for gold. The mountain had numerous large holes that had been dug or blasted and off from the base were tunnels with small buggy tracks still present. On weekends I would, alone, take my gear and rappel down these holes and explore the tunnels.

Upon returning to North Georgia my sophomore year, I continued this weekend activity as well as finding areas in Tallulah gorge to rappel. I also did these trips alone and on one occasion got stuck midair in a tree below where I began my descent, and it took me an hour or so to figure out how to get to the next ledge. By the end of fall quarter my sophomore year, I developed a low grade fever and what I would describe as mild respiratory flu symptoms. It was such that I decided not to go back to North Georgia for the winter quarter, thinking I could recuperate at home with the aid of my mother and grandmother. I enrolled at LaGrange College for the winter quarter so I stayed on course with my pre-med requirements. In retrospect, I probably contracted a fungal respiratory condition from the caves I was tramping around in. Years later I had a CT scan of my chest and abdomen in staging my prostate cancer and numerous granulomas were found in my chest and spleen, consistent with having had exposure to a fungal respiratory infection.

While I was at LaGrange College, something happened to me that I felt would be the ruination of my aspirations to become a doctor. One evening a friend and two girls I knew from high school accompanied me to Pizza Hut. It was not a date, it was more about me being back in LaGrange and socializing. We were all in my Ford Pinto and after eating, I went across the street to the parking lot of Roses. It was closed and I was pretending I couldn't get over speed bumps by revving the engine and then rolling back. It is something I enjoyed doing for people, I thought it was funny. Anyway I am in the midst of this and I look to my left to see two guys in a car asking me to roll down the window. I did and they were using horrible language and asking did I want to buy some "weed." I said no but they persisted and then began saying words that were purposely offensive to the girls with us. I tried to leave but they followed along side of me. Finally, I told them to leave us alone and the next thing I knew I was getting out of my car. But before I could take a step, one of them had a knife to my neck. He began with threats to me and, without thinking, I hit him as hard as I could in the face. His knife went flying off. I followed him to the ground but before I could finish the deal, his friend hit me on the back of the head with a crow bar. I didn't feel it, but I felt and smelled the blood all over my face. I took the crow bar from him and by this time my friend was out of the car. Now we had the knife and the crow bar and we began to yell at them. I remember them being very pitiful looking and really, based on their size, shouldn't have been going around picking a fight. After some consultation with my friend and the girls, we decided to let them go and to give them their weapons back. I went to the Emergency Room for stitches. A low rent reporter for the paper read the doctor's account of the event, and the next day the LaGrange Daily News printed on the front page in bold letters, "Man Beaten." The man was me. Soon people were calling my mother not the least of which was the father of my girlfriend in

John C. McHugh M.D.

high school, who happened to be a judge, asking my mother what in the world was John doing in a parking lot fighting someone near midnight. I did not feel my quest for medical school would survive this, but it did give me a renewed interest of getting out of LaGrange and going back to Dahlonega. As a side note, as the two assailants were leaving and after I had found my glasses, I memorized their license plate number. When I told my mother the whole story and that I had the plate numbers she said, "I want to see the little punks!" She called the police and gave them the information and in about an hour we were invited to the police station to identify them and decide if we wanted to press charges. Mother and I just looked at them for a minute and one of their mothers said, "I don't know why my son is in trouble, it's his face that is messed up."

Satisfied my mother said, "I don't need to charge them with anything, I just wanted to look at them." I must say they were pitiful to look at.

As a result of my unintended notoriety, I was excited about returning to North Georgia in the Cadet Corp and getting back into my pre-med curriculum. One of the classes that quarter was invertebrate biology and a new situation for me as it was a night class. In the class was the cocky student from Chickamauga I have previously alluded to. It wasn't long before I learned of our common goal of becoming a doctor, that his grades needed major improving, and that we had numerous similar interests, particularly sports. Tony had money. I did not have money. Tony had a nice new beautiful maroon and white 1973 Pontiac LeMans. Tony was very unselfish. Up until Tony, I did not have a true friend in college other than acquaintances in the dorm or others walking to the chow hall for meals. Until Tony, I could count on one hand eating anywhere other than the chow hall for every meal. Until Tony, I had never travelled to Gainesville, thirty miles south of Dahlonega, for anything other than seeing a doctor for a broken nose I got playing football. Right off the bat, we were eating out after the biology class, playing basketball and tennis together, trout fishing, and strategizing about getting into medical school. I think Tony appreciated my grades and my discipline in studying and our association was a positive influence on him; a perk to the relationship one might say. We were good for each other. If I declined eating out at a restaurant in Gainesville, he would quickly say I did not have worry about gas and he'd happily pay for the meal. To my knowledge Tony made nothing but A's once he decided he needed to get serious. Tony was very competitive so anything you did with him, whether it was being in the same class, playing tennis, or dating, it was always done in this context. All of these things I was doing with Tony made me a more confident person; friendships do this. I uncharacteristically decided to run for the upcoming year's Student Government Association Junior Class Vice President and won. Spring quarter of my sophomore year was the first time I had had both a productive and good time in college and as it ended, I looked forward to returning in the fall. I owe this to having met Tony. Both Tony and I had plans to be orderlies that summer in our respective home town hospitals as part of our plan to get into medical school.

When we returned to North Georgia, we were in the same Cadet Corp Company, Echo Company, and were roommates. Tony and I were in the same fraternity, Sigma Nu. Although I had pledged Sigma Nu at the tail end of my freshman year, I was not engaged in the activities until I starting being friends with Tony. I have often said that my junior year in college was one of the best years of my life. Tony and I were playing tennis, doing all the fraternity activities, my grades were good, and then I met and began dating Karen, my future wife. I made the North Georgia Soccer team despite having never played soccer. I became a starting halfback and lettered. I thoroughly enjoyed travelling to other colleges in the school bus and playing.

Dr. John Owen, the president of North Georgia at the time, invited the Student Government representatives to the president's house for dinner and to meet everyone. Although I am sure there were other influences, I asked him if he was aware that the soccer team did not get letter jackets. He quickly said to me that he was unaware of that but that he could do something about it. Next thing the team knew, we were told that we would all be getting letter jackets, which we did. As you might guess, I still have my letter jacket from North Georgia and it is one my favorite possessions. A few days after the dinner with Dr. Owen and his wife, I wrote a small thank you note telling them how much we all appreciated the meal and his support of the SGA. Some fourteen years later, when I was a practicing urologist in Gainesville, and board member of the North Georgia Alumni Association, I attended my first meeting at the president's house; Dr. Owen was still the president at that time. After the meeting, Mrs. Owen approached me and told me she wanted to show me something. I followed her to the kitchen and on the wall was my thank-you note framed.

"John," Mrs. Owen said, "Do you recognize the signature there? John and I were so impressed that you took the time and effort to write a thank-you note to us. It was unusual." I remember saying to myself, "Thanks mother." She and grandmother were all about a hand written thank-you note.

I don't want to beat a dead horse but my junior year was hitting on all cylinders. Between the fraternity meetings and dances, the soccer, the SGA, playing on Echo Company's basketball team - I was having a social life I had never had and making great grades to boot. To top it off, the fraternity had a variety show every year called the Grin In. I did a Richard Pryor impersonation where he was a preacher and I had twenty or so fraternity members behind me in choir uniforms I had borrowed from the Baptist Church in Dahlonega. In another act, Tony and I and Bob Griffeth danced to the Andrews Sisters's "Boogie Woogie Bugle Boy" in the Holly Theater. I had hurt my knee playing basketball and did the dance in a cast. Returning home that summer, I had my second knee operation, the first as a result of a football injury to the other knee in high school, and after recovering was an orderly at West Georgia Medical Center.

My senior year Karen and I spent much more time together and Tony was given the position of Captain of Echo Company. This was an honor as it was unusual for a student in the Corp who was not committed to join the military to be given a leadership role. I was given a token position as a Battalion officer simply on the basis of my grades and I basically coasted militarily wise my senior year and drifted away from my fraternity friends to do things with Karen. My senior year was notable to me for three things: I got into medical school, I was voted Brother of the Year by my fraternity, and Karen and I went to the Sugar Bowl between The University of Georgia and The University of Pittsburgh in New Orleans. We went with Tony,

Jimmy Sauls and their girlfriends. To experience New Orleans on New Year's Eve having had limited exposure to that type of activity was liberating. As my mother would say, I "Saw how the other half lives."

I was accepted to medical school and Tony was not initially. Tony, after graduating from North Georgia, began a graduate program at the University of Georgia with the plan to reapply to medical school and in doing so was accepted for the next year. When Tony arrived in Augusta in the fall of 1982, I had been elected President of the sophomore class and had the honor of welcoming his class to MCG in their lecture hall. We decided to share the expenses of a small rental house a mile or so from campus. After two quarters, I moved out to live with two of my classmates just across the Savannah River in North Augusta, South Carolina, and Tony did a similar thing with people from his class. I married Karen after the first quarter of my senior year of medical school and I moved into her house on Ellis Street. As it happened, Tony and a mutual friend of ours, Clifton Hastings, subsequently moved into a rental home across the street and again we were neighbors. Tony was one of the first non family members to hold our first son, Clay.

I finished medical school and began my urological residency in Augusta. Tony and Clifton finished medical school the next year and did their cardiothoracic surgery residency in Charlotte, North Carolina, where they both stayed to practice. Before I met Tony, I had good grades but no social life. Tony had the social life but not the study habits. We both came along to each other at precisely the right time for our mutual benefit.

From left to right: Tony, Jimmy and me.

105

The MCAT

A s has been mentioned previously and duly noted by Dr. Davis, I don't test well. Not testing well does not bode well for the student wanting to get into medical school. Getting into medical school is the first obstacle to maneuver because you have to get into a medical school to begin the "doctor" journey. In general, this requires top of class type grades and testing well on the MCAT. Extracurricular activities are helpful if you are on the fence of acceptance and can distinguish you from a similarly qualified applicant. So here I was again being held hostage by a multiple choice test which was required to get into medical school, and knowing I would not do well on it.

In the spring of my junior year of college, I and a friend of mine who was also applying to medical school the next year went to Athens, Georgia, to take the test. We were in the motel room the night before and he began telling me he'd played basketball in high school and knowing that I had wrestled in high school challenged me to a wrestling match. "Wrestling can't be that much different from just being athletic," he told me. About thirty seconds later and after I let him go from being embarrassingly pinned he said, "I'll never question your wrestling abilities again." That was the only high point of my trip to Athens and taking the MCAT.

The scores come back and my friend did well above average despite having just above a 3.0 GPA and I, as expected, scored well below average despite a 3.8 GPA. As the quarter was ending and nearing time to return to LaGrange for the summer, I was devastated. I kept saying over and over to myself, "Why in the hell is my life dependent on damn multiple choice questions I can't study for?" And then it dawned on me that maybe I could study for the MCAT. With my financial situation, the idea of paying for a class to help me take the test, which is common today, was not an option and did not cross my mind. I went to the school book store and sure enough there was a book on how to study for the MCAT. It was about four hundred pages long, four inches thick, and cost me about four dollars. I decided that if I was going to get into medical school, this book was the key. I had the grades, I had the extracurricular activities, and it was clear all I needed was a better MCAT score.

That summer I worked at the LaGrange NAPA parts store just as I had most every summer since high school, except the summer I worked with my brother Cooper as a life guard at the "City Pool." After getting off at five from the NAPA store, I went home and ate. Two nights a week, I refereed Little League baseball from six to nine. The other nights of the week, and I mean every other night after work, I went to the Callaway Foundation library and studied the MCAT book. I divided the number of pages in the book by the anticipated days that I'd have before college started again and did that number of pages each time I was at the library. I would usually be there from six until it closed at nine. I enjoyed the routine and again, my lack of a social life or a girlfriend in LaGrange worked in my favor.

The book was clearly divided into vocabulary, analogies, reading a paragraph and then answering questions about it, and questions about the various maths. Math was primarily algebra, trigonometry, and geometry. The stuff in the book was not hard; it was as I began to note more about figuring out the rules of each section. The vocabulary was easy; that was just memorizing the definitions. The analogies had rules and reoccurring concepts that applied to all of them and in turn made them easier to figure out. The math I had had in high school and just had to relearn. The book was excellent and had explanations and techniques for mastering each section at the end of the book. To this day, I recall the hardest of all words for me to remember because it was spelled different than it sounded, but I mastered it. The word was "facetious." As the summer progressed, I worked through the book and about the time it was time to go back to school, I had finished it. I went through all of it so many times I could predict the direction the question was going and also determine what type of answer they were looking for. Each question became a game to me and it was fun to anticipate the answer. I suppose people who test well already have this gift, a gift that others of us have to struggle to achieve. As I went through the book, I began to notice things that had been on the MCAT I had previously taken and this too heightened my learning experience and helped me focus in on what the test deemed important. I don't remember any questions in the book or in the MCAT I had taken being in any of my science classes in college. There was no chemistry, biology, or physics. I found this odd, but in this too, the book helped me know what subject matter I should emphasize.

Back at school I signed up for the last opportunity to take the MCAT and still have time to include the score for the 1977 application process. Again, I went to Athens to take the test; however, I went alone as my friend did so well he did not need to take it again. This time all of the vocabulary words are familiar, the analogies all fit a pattern which I remembered, and the math was math...problems I'd done in the Callaway Foundation library. I left the testing area feeling very confident. The scores returned and although I did not "ace it" I did well above average and I felt my prospects for acceptance to medical school were going to be promising. I was accepted to the only school I applied to, the Medical College of Georgia in Augusta. It was one of the most satisfying days of my life and the culmination of four years of planning, preparation, achievement and...luck. Below is my acceptance letter to the Medical College of Georgia-a goal realized.

Mary Lynn Faress

T he summer after my junior year of college, I worked as an orderly at the West Georgia Medical Center in LaGrange, Georgia. I was very excited about the prospects of working at a hospital and getting to wear the all white orderly outfit with the white shoes. I was an orderly who floated, in other words I'd go into the nursing office each morning and they would assign me a floor. I usually either went to the medical fourth floor in the newer part of the hospital or to the second floor of the old building where the more chronically ill patients were. In either case, I spent my days giving baths, changing beds, and giving out and picking up meal trays. I worked at the hospital two summers so I interacted with the staff in the nursing office often. The head of nursing and my boss was Mary Lynn Faress. I'd show up, we'd swap salutations and she'd assign me a floor. On many occasions while getting my assignment, she'd ask if I wanted to do two shifts. To my knowledge I never declined, but I remember to this day the seven A to eleven P was a tough go of it. I'd had two knee surgeries; one from football and the other from a fraternity basketball game and the white shoes I had to wear were not forgiving to my knees. The money I made in the summer and during Christmas break supplemented the Callaway Foundation Scholarship money so the extra shifts and the overtime that entailed came in handy.

I took giving baths very seriously and made a point to scrub "every nook and cranny." I'd ask every older patient, "Did you know Robert Cooper Davis the pharmacist that owned Davis Pharmacy on the square?" The majority of the time they did and while I gave the bath, I got them to tell me how they knew him or something they may have known interesting about him. I was very proud of being related to the man who owned a pharmacy on the square. When we moved to LaGrange my grandfather had been dead for ten years, but the pharmacist that purchased the building kept the name Davis Pharmacy. So the name Davis was still on the building and that meant the world to me. In time, I was being called to other floors to give baths and at first I thought it was because I was doing such a good job. But it became apparent that I was doing somebody else's work they did not want to do. It got to the point that I was called away so often I did not have the time to do my own work.

One day the operating room called the floor and said they needed an orderly as soon as possible. One of the nurses told me to go to the operating room, change into scrubs, and go into the orthopedic room. I did not really know where the operating room was and I had never been in scrubs before, but it was very exciting. I was going to possibly meet a surgeon and see a surgery. I found the changing room and a nurse told me about which scrubs to use and pointed out the hats, masks, and shoe covers. I put all of it on and feeling very special went to the orthopedic room. There was a patient on the table who looked like he was going to have something done to his knee. They told me they needed me to hold the leg up by the ankle so the area could be cleaned. I lifted the ankle as instructed and as I did, the surgeon looked over at me with rage and said, "He has just contaminated the whole damn field, get him out of here!" They ushered me out, I changed back into my regular whites, and went back upstairs. Although I was crestfallen, I was not so naive to note that the surgeon was inappropriate. I made a pledge to myself in the elevator that if I were ever to "make a doctor" I would never treat someone the way he treated me. An hour or so later, the operating room called again for me to come down. I was ushered into the now empty orthopedic room with blood all over the floor, shown the mop and bucket, and instructed to clean it up. I found out the name of the orthopedic surgeon, I know his name as I write this, and I was determined to search him out when I was a surgeon to remind him of how he treated me. By the way, if he treated me that way, he was abusive to others. To this day, I disassociate myself from "better than thou" doctors; and make a point to be kind to all of the personnel of the various departments of the hospital. You would not believe the benefits of being in good stead with the employees of the dietary department!

I had numerous things happen to me when I was an orderly involving patients, co-workers, physicians, and the nurses. It was a 101 so to speak in the introduction to medicine. Mrs. Faress was my mentor through all this. Seeing me every morning, getting feedback from the nurses about the quality of my bath giving, and the number of double shifts I did when asked, Mrs. Faress knew my work ethic better than anyone. When I applied to medical school, I surprised my advisors by choosing her to do one of the two recommendations required in the application process. I firmly believe that my acceptance was bolstered by her letter.

Above the only picture I have in my "orderly whites" with my best friend in high school Weasel.

Virginia Tomlin

*O*ne of the things beneficial about our moving back to LaGrange was mother's extended family there. Since my grandfather had ten brothers and sisters and my grandmother had three sisters and a brother, I was related to half of Troup County. I was close with most of my aunts but Virginia was special for many reasons. She was a daughter of one of my grandfather's brothers. She had money and only one son and that son wore only the finest and trendiest of name brand clothing. At one time or another, eventually all five of us McHugh boys fit into Dave Tomlin's hand me downs. When I was Dave's size, Virginia would come over to our house about every three months with some clothes for me to try on. The jackets were London Fog, the shirts were Gant, the sport shirts were Lacrosse, nice ties, jackets, and I remember the very nice all wool shirts by Pendleton.

Mother would call upstairs and tell me that Virginia had dropped by to visit with clothing and to come down to the living room to go through them and try them on. "You tell Virginia you want them all and you and I will do the sorting out after she is gone. John, you don't look a gift horse in the mouth."

I'd go downstairs, go through the clothing, try on most of everything while mother, grandmother, and Virginia visited. Between their conversations each would at one time or another say, "That looks good John and it fits well too."

The clothes were in pristine condition and none looked like they had ever been worn. All had been professionally laundered and the shirts had a name tag on the inside the back collar that read, "Dave Tomlin." I wore these clothes in high school, college, medical school, residency, and finally relinquished the last Lacrosse shirt after starting private practice fifteen years later. I had a fraternity brother in college who needed to borrow one of my shirts for some function he was attending. He picked one out and wore it that evening and brought it back the next day. Giving me the shirt he said, "Thanks John, by the way who is Dave Tomlin?"

When I finished college, Virginia came over to our house and gave me a hundred dollars. "John I want you to buy yourself a suit."

It was the most money anyone had ever given me to that point in my life. I did not however buy a suit with the money despite my mother telling me repeatedly, "John you need to buy you a nice suit." I did however keep a suit of Dave's that I had gotten from Virginia, which I wore on my wedding day.

John Rice Hudson

John Hudson was the most popular person in my medical school class - and for good reason. Besides being a jack of all trades, the guy had the biggest heart in the world. He availed himself to anyone who needed help...with anything. He commonly wore Dickie work uniforms and his shirt had his first name on a white label above the front pocket. He must have worked for a mechanic shop through college, but it did not stop there. He could fix washing machines and anything mechanical that a fellow student had that didn't work. He carried all of his tools and jumper cables in his car at all times. I can recount numerous times seeing him in the parking lot jumping a car off or getting into an accidently locked car. Our class did not call the campus security for a dead battery - we called John.

He also played a wide array of instruments, particularly the trombone. His claim to fame early on in medical school involved how he announced an upcoming class party. Whoever was going to have a party would ask him to get the word out to the class. So on the Friday before the party, John would come into our lecture hall in the middle of a professor's lesson playing the instrument of choice as loud as his windpipes would allow. As I recall, on one occasion he came in with a bass drum. When he had everyone's attention he'd stop and then announce the details of the upcoming party. I never remember a professor complaining or appearing annoyed. I think they marvelled at his chutzpah. The whole class loved him.

What I liked about him was that there was no attempt on his part to be anything other than who he was. The clothes he wore were employee issue from a mechanic shop, he made no pretense that he was trying to make good grades, and he disarmed you with just unselfish goodness. Although I was not close friends with John outside of school, I did socialize with him during classes and at class parties.

Each year the freshman class at the Medical College of Georgia put on a talent show of sorts; it was a tradition. I am a big Beatle fan and I took the song "When I'm Sixty-Four" and changed the lyrics to fit a struggling medical student. The chorus became, "I'll still be in medical school when I'm sixty-four." John got the sheet music for it and he and I danced to the song with the new lyrics while a classmate played the piano. It is one of my fondest memories.

On one occasion near the end of our senior year, John needed a ride somewhere and I had an opportunity to catch up with him about his plans after graduation.

"John, I am going to join the Navy. The benefits package for a Navy intern is much better than the traditional schools and after one year I'll be an officer as a Family Medicine doctor." He then went on to tell me about other benefits, salary and how he looked forward to travelling. In a way, I was envious of him as my education path had been four years of college, four years of medical school, and then the anticipated five years of residency - all in Georgia without any interval between the various stages.

Our class graduated and everyone dispersed all over America pursuing different specialties in a myriad of residency programs. Although John did his Family Practice internship in Augusta, I had very little contact with him. That was 1982 and one day out of the blue, about a year or so later, I received a postcard from John. I know I would have saved the card and was surprised it wasn't in my Juicy Fruit box, but despite hours of searching, I cannot find it...but I will. It had a beautiful Mediterranean scene on the front with a seaside view of columns and palm trees and in the background what appeared ancient structures.

On the back of the card John had written, "Hi John, hope you are well. You'll never guess where I am now...Beirut, Lebanon. I am the only medical doctor for the Marines here. This place doesn't look like the picture on the front of this card anymore. There's lots of rubble. Anyway I hope you are doing okay and I know you are excited about starting your urology residency," John.

A few months later, on October 23, 1983, a Hezbollah terrorist drove a truck with 2,000 pounds of explosives into the US military compound near the Beirut airport and detonated it. The attack killed 241 service members including 220 Marines. It was the deadliest attack on the Marines since the battle for Iwo Jima in War World II in 1945. John Hudson died that day. I have since read that he had a six month old child at the time of his death.

I think I have read somewhere that really good people, people who have been an example for others, uplifted others and have always been kind to others regardless of their status have made such an impact that they don't need a long life. This observation fits John Hudson and I am a better person for having known him. I can see him now with his light blue Dickies shirt with his name tag on it playing his trombone, fixing washing machines, and jumping off cars with dead batteries in heaven.

Dr. W.

M y strategy to get into medical school was to go to a small military school in North Georgia, make good grades, and participate in extracurricular activities. I strongly felt that having gone to a military school, I would potentially stand out from all the students applying from the University of Georgia. Where we had about five students applying for medical school from North Georgia College, the University of Georgia probably had a hundred or more.

I was able to make good grades; I minored in English Literature to further differentiate myself from all the science type students, I lettered in Soccer, was an officer in the Cadet Corp, I was Vice President of the SGA, and was an officer in my fraternity and elected Brother of the Year. I have mentioned that I was able to bring my MCAT scores up, so I felt my chances were good and all was working to plan. Part of the medical school admissions was to go to Augusta for interviews; one with a practicing physician associated with the Medical College of Georgia, and the second with one of the professors. The girl I was dating at the time, and now my wife, lived in Augusta, so we were able to visit her parents, and I'd have a place to stay during the interviews.

The first interview was with a female professor. She was very nice and asked softball questions. I believe she did interviews but was not on the admissions committee. She probably reported highlights of the interview and her recommendation to the admissions committee. The second interview was the most important one and the one with the most to win or lose. The interviewer was Dr. Roy Witherington. He was on the admissions committee, Chairman of the Department of Urology, and very formal and straight-laced. He was in his fifties, his hair was very short, and he was wearing a perfectly white, heavily starched cotton clinical jacket. He had, to me, the look of a very conservative, no nonsense, but polite and gentlemanly air about him.

My first impression was that my plan about going to a military school and then getting someone like Dr. Witherington was just perfect. The typical student from UGA most probably would have had long hair. His questions were similar to the previous interview.

"Why do you want to be a doctor John?"

I had the perfect answer for this and it was the truth and I believe it was a good answer. "My mother had five boys and several miscarriages and through the years she interacted with numerous doctors. Many of the doctors became friends of hers. She spoke so highly of them and in such admiration and gratitude. It dawned on me at an early age that in being a doctor, I could make a living and help people at the same time. I wanted to be the doctor my mother saw in her doctors. With everything my mother has been through, I feel my becoming a doctor may in a small way give her back some respect and repay all she has done for me."

I got into medical school probably in large part to a favorable recommendation from Dr. Witherington. The third and forth years of medical school are clinical based and are done at the hospital. During this time, I rotated through urology and got to know Dr. W., as he was called by the residents, from the perspective of treating patients. Whereas internal medicine was difficult for me to grasp, urology to me was very simple. It has the benefit of being a surgical subspecialty with limited exposure to after-hours emergencies. This, in addition to being able to take hospital call from home, made my decision of what type of doctor I wanted to become easy.

During my senior year of medical school, I applied to the Medical College of Georgia's urology residency program. It was the only residency program I applied to as I wanted to stay in Augusta. I mistakenly thought that Dr. W. had one of the two spots for the program for me. I knew that he had given one to a fellow classmate of mine from Augusta and whose father was a local pediatrician. My friend as well already had a spot with Augusta's leading urology group after completing his residency. In fact, Dr. W. had offered the spot to several other applicants from high-powered medical schools with much higher medical school grades and credentials than mine. I was probably about his fifth or so choice. One day I went by to see Dr. W. and asked where he was in the process of naming the new urology residents. I assumed he would tell me then that I'd be one of them.

"John where else have you applied for residency?"

"MCG is the only one Dr. W."

"John that was not very wise. Well, if it doesn't work out, I can find you a place somewhere. I'll speak to a friend of mine in Mississippi; there may be a spot there for you."

I remember going home thinking what in the world will I do if I have to pack up everything and move to Mississippi? Mississippi? Why hadn't I applied to more than one residency? The fact was I just had a feeling it would work out. Miraculously, after a few weeks I got a call from Dr. W. telling me that I was in the program. I had probably told my mother about my situation and her praying for me did the trick. Growing up mother would kneel at my bedside each night and pray. This continued whenever I was home until I married.

So a happenchance interview with a member of the admissions committee was instrumental in getting me into medical school, who happens to be the Chairman of Urology and who happens to give me a spot in his program in Augusta. Then of course I benefited by being in his program and learning urology in a program that had his finger prints all over it.

Dr. W. had a saying that we as residents would repeat often and applies to my luckily staying in Augusta to do my residency, "Boys...everything is going to be alright."

Dr. W. is second from the right on the front row.

John C. McHugh M.D.

My Damn Eyes

Fourth Grade, Columbus, Georgia: My teacher figured out, not me or my family, that I could not see. I remember going down to Pearle Vision with my mother in downtown Columbus. It was a small and narrow shop and at the time, with all the attention I was getting, I felt important and happy to be getting glasses. I remember returning to our home on Flint Drive, getting out of the Ford Falcon station wagon, and looking at the tree across the street that housed our tree house. It was amazing seeing individual leaves. Up until this point, I thought all trees from a distance were a mass of green. From this time, until I was a freshman at North Georgia College in Dahlonega, Georgia, I got a newer and stronger pair of glasses every six months. My poor mother would pay five dollars a month in an attempt to stay current with expenses associated with the glasses. I was very nearsighted: Coke-a-cola bottle nearsighted. I learned from experience to refuse any classmate's request to look through my glasses. The resultant knee-jerk response of, "Oh my God, you're blind!" became old and embarrassing very quickly and all future requests denied.

Jump ahead to me being a first year urology resident. The strength of my glasses was such that they did not mesh with the lenses in the cystoscope. Cystoscopy is the most common and important procedure a urologist performs. All I could see when I inserted the scope was blurry red. I thought this was normal. My first cystoscopy at the VA resulted in a bladder perforation and even when this happened, I did not know it. It took another resident to figure out what I had done. The fact that I couldn't see became the topic of conversation of all the residents. It was a depressing time for me, as I thought there would be a chance I'd have to choose a new residency. I stopped attempting doing cystoscopies and would find ways to have someone else do them for me. To my attendings' credit, if they knew what was going on with me, they never questioned me about the issue. This was in keeping with Dr. Witherington's overall philosophy of, "It will be all right."

120

Then I got the idea that maybe the clash between my glasses and the lens of the cystoscope could be corrected by another lens. I got a thirty degree lens from one of the cystoscopes and took it down to the ophthalmology department and explained what was going on, and thankfully, they were very helpful. They tried a series of hand held lenses interposed between me and scope, and in time we found a power that worked. They gave me this red lens holder that I adapted to the cystoscope. I then found out that Storz made a clip-on device for the scope that you could put the power lens in you needed. (Obviously, this was a problem for others.)
So, for three years, I never went anywhere without my clip-on "rectifier." It worked like a charm. That thing saved my career.

After starting private practice, soft contact lenses improved to the point that I could wear them. For some reason, wearing contacts corrected the cystoscope issue. About this time, as well, the flexible cystoscope with an adjustable focus and the use of cameras for the cystoscope made looking directly into the eyepiece obsolete. Today, all of the operating rooms have large adjustable monitors attached to ceiling and hi tech cameras to attach to the scopes making all of the above history moot. So, in the end, it all worked out. Life is funny that way.
Dr. Witherington was right after all: "It will be all right."

My "Rectifier."

Spring of my freshman year I had it in my head that I wanted to go through Marine Officer Training in Quantico, Virginia. I met with a Marine officer, hiked a portion of the Appalachian Trail with other aspiring marines, and even took a placement test to see if I qualified academically. Once all this was done, I was told to go to a military base, as I remember somewhere near Warner Robbins, to have a physical exam. If you wonder how this was going to fit in with going to medical school, it didn't. I just wanted to go through the training. I love obstacle courses. Well, my eyes were so bad the Marines wouldn't have me for the reason of "defective visual acuity; excessive refractive error." They even destroyed my enlistment papers. Ironically, my niche in urology is doing a surgery very few urologists do and that is microscopic vasectomy reversals. The procedure takes about two hours and utilizes an operating microscope to place 12-14 microscopic sutures each the size of a strand of hair to reconnect the vas deferens. The opening in the vas that is reattached is the size of the "o" in God on a penny.

I mention this story to emphasize that you too will be thwarted in achieving something you want. You have to just keep the old head up and keep plugging away remembering that, "When the world gives you lemons...make lemonade!"

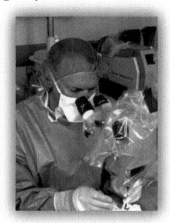

DEPARTMENT OF THE NAVY
HEADQUARTERS UNITED STATES MARINE CORPS
WASHINGTON, D.C. 20380

IN REPLY REFER TO
MMRE-32-U-mad
10 July 1974

Mr. John C. McHugh
103 North Lewis Street
LaGrange, Georgia 30240

Dear Mr. McHugh:

The Chief, Bureau of Medicine and Surgery, Department of the Navy, after a review of your report of physical examination informed this Headquarters that you do not meet the physical requirements for enrollment in the Platoon Leaders Class Program by reason of "defective visual acuity; excessive refractive error."

In view of the above, your application for enrollment is disapproved, your conditional enlistment in the Marine Corps Reserve is voided and the enlistment papers in your case have been destroyed. You are now under no contractual obligation to the U. S. Marine Corps.

In view of your interest in obtaining commissioned grade in the Marine Corps Reserve, it is regretted that this action is necessary.

Sincerely,

P. E. TUCKER,
Major, U. S. Marine Corps
Recruitment Branch
By direction of the Commandant of the Marine Corps

Copy to:
OSO Atlanta
Dir, 6th MCD

"You do not meet the physical requirements for enrollment in the Platoon Leaders Class Program by reason of *"defective visual acuity; excessive refractive error."* In view of the above, your application for enrollment is disapproved, your conditional enlistment in the Marines Corps Reserve is voided and your enlistment papers in your case have been destroyed. In view of your interest in obtaining commissioned grade in the Marine Corps Reserve, it is regretted that this action is necessary."

Janice Watts

I had been involved in a Ponzi Scheme and lost a boat load of money and was having trouble sleeping. I would wake up at 5 a.m. every morning without fail and couldn't go back to sleep. After about a month of this, I decided I'd get up when I woke up regardless of the time and begin writing. My first plan was to write a book about things that had happened to me and tie it in to a phrase my mother used to say all the time, "We can't have nothing!" One story involved running out of gas on the way to the beach to stay at a condo we owned in Orange Beach, Alabama. I was driving my wife's Range Rover and didn't note the low fuel gauge and we ran out of gas just south of Montgomery. My college aged daughter was with us and was quite exasperated about being stuck on the side of the road in ninety degree heat. It took three hours before someone came with gas. When we finally got to Orange Beach, I determined that the rental agent had rented our condo without my knowledge so we had nowhere to stay. The essence of this story was the final line, "Now I got something, but still I can't have nothing."

During one of our trips to Orange Beach, we were walking at Johnson Beach and realized we did not have any sun screen. I walked up to the next person I saw on the beach and asked if we could borrow a couple of squirts of lotion. The lady was under an umbrella reading, in her late sixties and the lotion she gave me was circa 1960 Coppertone sun tanning lotion.

I look at the container and said, "Wow I haven't seen this stuff in a while."

She said, "It still works."

My wife and I put the stuff on and said thanks and she asked where we were from, and this began a conversation. It turned out she was living in Pensacola and came to this particular spot, Crossover C, to read and write on a regular basis. We learned that she was a widower, a retired English Literature professor, and was beginning to write her memoir. I mentioned that I was writing, but I didn't know grammar. I said that I always wanted to write a book but the grammar thing had held me back; recalling the "F" I made in my last English class.

"That's the easy part John," she said confidently.

My wife chirped in, "Yeah John, you never separate a period from the sentence by a quotation mark."

"John," the lady continued, "the grammar part I can do for you. I can be your editor if you want to write a book."

We decide that I'd send her by email my stories that I had written and others as they were completed. She would correct them and send them back to me. This perchance meeting on Johnson Beach lead me to fulfilling a goal I wanted to attain all of my adult life, that being writing and publishing a book. Over the next several months, I wrote about everything I thought was interesting about things that had happened to me with the twist that every story had a sort of Rodney Dangerfield feel to it. Instead of "I get no respect" my shtick was "I can't have nothing."

One morning I was thinking of another story to begin and it dawned on me that it would be easy to write a book on prostate cancer. The angle was not to be overly medical but to emphasize the decision making process. It was a novel idea as most books are informative but don't break down the process of determining which treatment, if any, one should pursue. I had been through the process myself, having been treated for prostate cancer, and I had guided probably a thousand or so patients through the process. I was indeed an "expert." I also could draw pictures for the book that I used on the exam room table paper over the years. I mentioned to Janice, my editor, that I was changing direction. I told her I felt I could put together the prostate book quickly, and that I already "had it in my head." When I sent her the first installment of my book, she wrote back that she felt she was not qualified to be the editor of a medical book. She felt I should get someone else and after going back and forth on the matter, we both agreed on me getting another editor.

I worked on the book over the next several months, using what grammar and punctuation skills I had, and finished the rough draft. All the while I was working with the son of a friend who had taken some graphic design classes in college and who was familiar with Adobe Illustrator. He took my rough drawings and used Illustrator to clean them up. I found an editor on line who had some medical background and after about three months the book was sent back to me corrected. I gave this version to a friend who was an English teacher at Brenau University, and she polished it a bit further. I then had my Practice Administrator teach me how to do some formatting of the paragraphs and the information above each page, like my name and the title of the book. For the cover, I called a patient of mine who is a very talented photographer and he obligingly invited me to his studio to have pictures taken at no cost. My idea was to portray me as the physician and a patient. So the cover has me holding a path report for prostate cancer in one hand and emanating out of my scrubs are catheter tubing and a drainage bag full of what looks like urine. The "urine" depicted was actually a mixture of a Bud Light and a Heineken. The Bud Light alone was too light but the Heineken made the urine concentration and color just right.

After all this was done, I used Microsoft Word to make text boxes to highlight various aspects of the book and for quotes. The book became a collection of aphorisms, illustrations, personal stories, and just the right touch of real medical talk about prostate cancer. I used Createspace.com, an on line print on demand company, to print and publish the book. The book has been in the top ten on Amazon for the topic of prostate cancer since its publication in 2010.

To market the book, I created a blog about prostate cancer using Wordpress. I'd write a blog post about prostate cancer decision making and the politics of prostate cancer several times a week. I used as my media pictures I'd taken of my dogs, landscape, and fishing. The pictures I'd use would have nothing to do with the content I was writing about; in other words, it was a site where one could learn something about prostate cancer in an informal and comfortable way. I put in excerpts from my book, I made a video of me and my Chocolate Lab Penelope for the Amazon author page, and in time I had done several hundred blog posts.

As of November 2017, there have been over one million views of my Prostate Diaries blog and it is one of the most viewed sites on prostate cancer in America.

All of this because of the odd assimilation of losing hundreds of thousands of dollars in a Ponzi Scheme, coming down with prostate cancer, and being encouraged by meeting a random retired English Professor to pursue a lifelong goal. When people ask me how I was able to get a book published I say, "There's nothing to it!"

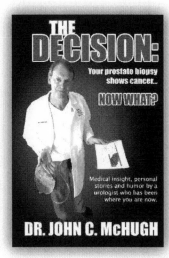

Karen

T he idea of this book started when I was looking through an old Juicy Fruit box of things I had saved over the years and found my high school graduation speech. In looking through all the letters, I found several from my current wife and then girl friend when we were dating. One of the letters was addressed to "My Little Doctor." What is important about this and other letters I saved during college is that I found encouraging letters from a lot of people I had forgotten had been a part of my becoming a doctor. There was one from my little brother Jeff with the note, "I have enclosed two dollars so you can get to college and back." One from my older brother Cooper informed me about his having gotten me a life guarding job at the City Pool that summer. A very nice note from Cooper's wife, Beverly, encouraging me and assuring me that I could achieve anything I set my mind to. The bank document showing where Rushton's first wife, Shelia, who worked as a secretary at a local bank, had co-signed a two thousand dollar loan for a Ford Pinto I had purchased. Of course there were numerous letters from my mother and grandmother. There was a letter with money from my brother Bob when he started work and I was still in school. I could go on. If you look around, you will see that a lot of people have helped make you who you are and are still supporting you.

When Karen referred to me as "My Little Doctor", I had not gotten into medical school. Everybody and their brother in my freshman class were going to be doctors. I remember being introduced to Karen's parents when I was a junior and how unimpressive it sounded to say that I was "pre- med." That didn't really mean anything. I probably wouldn't get in; if I did I might not have the wherewithal to finish medical school and then the whole residency thing. The "I'm going to be a doctor" and actually practicing medicine was nine years away.

My children over the years have said to their mother, "I bet it was a no brainer to date dad knowing he was going to be a doctor." She didn't know I'd be a doctor, but she did have confidence in me and encouraged me "before" my acceptance to medical school. It doesn't stop there. She married someone with no job and no certainty that having a physician as a husband would come to fruition. I had no income and paid for medical school with a fifty thousand dollar loan I received from a state program to encourage medical students to practice in small communities. I signed papers assuring them that fourteen years later I would be in a town less than twenty thousand people although I didn't know what kind of doctor I'd be. If I didn't do what I said, the money would be expected to be paid back in full at the point I reneged. None of this bothered me. I needed the money having gotten into medical school with no clue how I'd pay for it. So when we married, Karen signed on for that debt knowing also that there were no financial resources from my family to rely on. Karen was an art teacher and worked at a junior high school before and after we married. I moved into Karen's house on Ellis St. near Lake Olmstead her parents had purchased for her at the cost of twenty thousand dollars. The house had one bedroom, one bath, and a space heater that emanated from the floor. One had to step over it in the winter or it burned your feet. It was conveniently located in a hallway right in front of the bathroom door making negotiating it a common occurrence.

We got married in December 1979, and we had our first child in November, 1980. Go ahead count the number of months, everyone does. Karen continued to work until I was an intern and then began staying at home to be a full-time mom. The salary for surgical interns was approximately eighteen thousand dollars a year, so between the salary and the loan, we got by. During the second year of residency, I was able to "moonlight" in the emergency rooms of small community hospitals making about a thousand dollars a weekend. I worked in several, but my most common location was Millen, Georgia. Once a month, I'd leave Talmadge Hospital after work on a Friday and drive to

Millen eating a Burger King chicken sandwich on the way and getting there by six. I'd then work until Monday a.m. and then drive home to shower and be at work at the hospital by eight. The call schedule for a surgical intern required taking and staying at the hospital every third night so on those days I'd go to work at seven in morning and return home thirty-six hours later. The every third night call mingled in with the once a month weekend tour in Millen was a bit much on several fronts.

I have taken the time to painstakingly explain my schedule as a resident not on my account but on Karen's. Before you start feeling sorry for the poor chap going through a residency program, what about the lovely wife. Can you just imagine all of the time she was not only alone, but alone taking care of a child? We had our second child in 1983 and so now she had a newborn, a three year old, and every third night and every fourth weekend she was by herself taking care of the home front. Acknowledging this is why those of us having gone through it don't take so well to the new doctor leaving the wife of his residency once he has "made it." Karen is as responsible for my becoming a doctor as I am. And here's the thing and in keeping with how she is today...she never complained, she only supported and encouraged.

The take away? You may not know it, but you too have a Karen and you must be careful to remember that you will not get to where you want to be without the help of others. Thinking you are going to do anything by yourself is prideful; one needs to emphasize being grateful. It starts with recognizing it and that takes some observant reflection. A word to the wise is sufficient.

And I know your image of me is what I hope to be. -Leon Russell "A Song for You"

*The only difference between the saint and the
sinner is that every saint has a past, and every
sinner has a future.
-Oscar Wilde*

The Past-Leave it but learn from it.

> *That means a lot, the ones who love you*
> *because they are the ones who got you*
> *here and it is their effect on your past*
> *which will determine your future.*
> *Think about that.*

I t takes a wise man to learn from his mistakes, but even a wiser man to learn from others.
-Zen Proverb

Forget what hurt you but never forget what it taught you.
-Anonymous

Remember, today is the tomorrow you worried about yesterday.
-Dale Carnegie

Good judgment comes from experience, and a lot of that comes from bad judgment.
-Will Rogers

You'll never get ahead of anyone as long as you try to get even with him.
-Lou Holtz

Never let yesterday use up too much of today.
-Will Rogers

How unhappy is he who cannot forgive himself.
-Publilius Syrus

The best remedy for an injury is to forget it.
-Publilius Syrus

Yesterday ended last night. Today is a brand-new day.
-Zig Ziglar

Make the present good, and the past will take care of itself.
-Knute Rockne

Yesterday is history, tomorrow is a mystery, today is a gift of
God, which is why we call it the present.
-Bil Keane

Tomorrow is the most important thing in life. Comes into us at
midnight very clean. It's perfect when it arrives and it puts itself
in our hands. It hopes we've learned something from yesterday.
-John Wayne

Never regret anything because at one time it was exactly what
you wanted.
-Marilyn Monroe

What is uttered is finished and done with.
-Thomas Mann

You do indeed have a past, but not now! And, yes, you have a
future, but not now! You can consume your now with thoughts
of 'then' and 'maybe,' but that will keep you from the inner peace
you could experience.
-Wayne Dyer

The beginning of wisdom is this: Get wisdom. Though it cost all
you have, get understanding.
-Proverb 4:7

Learn how to be happy with what you have while you pursue all
that you want.
-John Rohn

Live out of your imagination, not your history. -Stephen Covey

John C. McHugh M.D.

Experience is the teacher of all things.
-Julius Caesar

Experience is simply the name we give our mistakes.
-Oscar Wilde

Don't look back. Something might be gaining on you.
-Satchel Paige

You can't unscramble eggs.
-J.P. Morgan

It's fine to celebrate success but it is more important to heed the
lessons of failure. -Bill Gates

Time ripens all things; no man is born wise.
-Miguel de Cervantes

Live out of your imagination, not your history. -Stephen Covey

Wisdom consists of the anticipation of consequences.
-Norman Cousins

Tears water our growth.
-William Shakespeare

Good judgement is the result of experience and experience the
result of bad judgement.
-Mark Twain

Experience is a great teacher...it helps me recognize my mistakes
the second time.
-Anonymous

By seeking and blundering we learn.
-Johann Wolfgang von Goethe

We are products of our past, but we don't have to be prisoners
of it.
-Rick Warren

I regret to this day that I never went to college.
I feel I should have been a doctor.
-Ty Cobb

Think Long Term - Don't choose short-term gratification over long-term gain.

> A lot of hope has been placed on your education.
> They realize the long-term gain involved.

Maturity is achieved when a person postpones immediate pleasures for long-term values.
-Joshua L. Liebman

Luck is what happens when preparation meets opportunity.
-Seneca

Imitation is suicide.
-Ralph Waldo Emerson

It is easier to find men who will volunteer to die, than to find those who are willing to endure pain with patience.
-Julius Caesar

The most reliable way to predict the future is to create it.
-Abraham Lincoln

Opportunity dances with those who are ready on the dance floor. -H. Jackson Brown

It's hard for young players to see the big picture. They just see three or four years down the road.
-Kareem Abdul-Jabbar

I don't think anyone is thinking long-term now.
-Thomas Mann

My own view is that every company requires a long-term view.
-Jeff Bezos

You can't grow long-term if you can't eat short-term. Anybody can manage short. Anybody can manage long. Balancing those two things is what management is.
-Jack Welch

Long-term sustainable change happens if people discover their own power.
-Pierre Omidyar

Do more than you are being paid to do, and you'll eventually be paid more for what you do.
-Zig Ziglar

As I grow older, I pay less attention to what men say. I just watch what they do.
-Andrew Carnegie

You have to decide what your highest priorities are and have the courage-pleasantly, smilingly, nonapologetically, to say "no" to other things. And the way you do that is by having a bigger "yes" burning inside. The enemy of the "best" is often the "good.
-Stephen Covey

Nobody ever did, or ever will, escape the consequences of his choices. -Alfred Armand Montapert

You must have long term goals to keep you from being frustrated by short term failures.
-Charles C. Nobel

The ability to discipline yourself to delay gratification in the short term in order to enjoy greater returns in the long term is the indispensible perquisite for success.
-Maxwell Maltz

We have two ears and one mouth so that we can listen twice as much as we speak.
-Epictetus

Learn to Listen-If you're talking you ain't learning.

> *Let's take for instance the simple art of communication. What if we could not communicate with our peers in matters of importance ranging from gossip to politics?*

L isten with the intent to understand, not the intent to reply.
-Stephen Covey

Courage is what it takes to stand up and speak; courage is also what it takes to sit down and listen.
-Winston Churchill

I like to listen. I have learned a great deal from listening carefully. Most people never listen.
-Ernest Hemingway

Listen to many, speak to a few.
-William Shakespeare

Older and wiser voices can help you find the right path, if you are only willing to listen.
-Jimmy Buffett

Speak little and to the purpose.
-American Proverb

Don't be afraid of enemies who attack you. Be afraid of the friends who flatter you.
- Dale Carnegie

You never really understand a person until you consider things from his point of view...Until you climb inside of his skin and walk around in it.
-Harper Lee

You can make more friends in two months by becoming interested in other people than you can in two years by trying to get other people interested in you.
-Dale Carnegie

Grown-ups never understand anything by themselves, and it is tiresome for children to be always and forever explaining things to them.
-Antoine de Saint-Exupéry

Silence is one of the great arts of conversation.
-Marcus Tullius Cicero

Young men, hear an old man to whom old men hearkened when he was young.
-Augustus

Silence is a true friend who never betrays.
-Confucius

Let the wise hear and increase in learning, and the one who understands obtain guidance
-Proverbs 1:5

Fools despise wisdom and instruction. -Solomon

Listen, my son, to your father's instruction and do not forsake your mother's teaching.
-Proverbs 1:8

I often regret that I have spoken; never that I have been silent.
-Publilius Syrus

The most important thing in communication is hearing what isn't said. -Peter Drucker

But far more numerous was the herd of such, who think too
little, and who talk too much.
-John Dryden

Brevity is the soul of wit.
-Shakespeare

Mediocrity can talk, but it is for genius to observe.
-Benjamin Disraeli

One reason why a dog is such a lovable creature is that his tail
wags instead of his tongue.
-Anonymous

Some people talk to animals. Not many listen though. That's the
problem.
-Winnie-the-Pooh

It was impossible to get a conversation going, everybody was
talking too much.
-Yogi Berra

Your most unhappy customers are your greatest source of
learning.
-Bill Gates

It takes a great man to be a listener. -Calvin Coolidge

Men of few words are the best men. -William Shakespeare

Listening, not imitation, may be the sincerest form of flattery.
-Joyce Brothers

The tongue of the wise commends knowledge, but the mouth of
the fool gushes folly. -Proverbs 15:2

A wise man takes council of his friends.
-Shakespeare

You can observe a lot by just watching. -Yogi Berra

Employ your time in improving yourself by other men's writings so that you shall come easily by what others have laboured hard for.
-Socrates

The Power of Biographies and History-Study the lives of famous people.

> *Clark Gable had everything, except education. He admitted it and tried hard to convince young people of its importance. After explaining the whys and so forth he would always end with this tale. He said that whenever he was at a party or some social gathering and the group at which he was standing would start an intelligent conversation he would say, "Excuse me please" and then go to the men's room. As a result he said he spent one third of his life going to the men's room, one third of it in the men's room and one third coming back.*

I 'm just a lucky slob from Ohio who happened to be in the right place at the right time.
-Clark Gable

Read no history: nothing but biography, for that is life without theory.
-Benjamin Disraeli

There is nothing new in the world except the history you do not know.
-Harry S. Truman

If you read enough biography and history, you learn how people have dealt successfully or unsuccessfully with similar situations or patterns in the past. It doesn't give you a template of answers, but it does help you refine the questions you have to ask yourself.
-James Mattis

Biography is the only true history.
-Thomas Carlyle

All history is biography.
-Ralph Waldo Emerson

Biography lends to death a new terror.
-Oscar Wilde

I only read biographies, metaphysics and psychology. I can dream up my own fiction.
-Mae West

There ain't nothing that breaks up homes, country and nations like somebody publishing their memoirs
-Will Rogers

We are not makers of history. We are made by history.
-Martin Luther King, Jr.

A people without the knowledge of their past history, origin and culture is like a tree without roots.
-Marcus Garvey

Those who do not remember the past are condemned to repeat it. -George Santayana

History, despite its wrenching pain, cannot be unlived, but if faced with courage, need not be lived again.
-Maya Angelou

A house without books is like a room without windows.
-Horace Mann

History will be kind to me for I intend to write it.
-Winston Churchill

History is a gallery of pictures in which there are few originals
and many copies.
-Alexis de Tocqueville

A library is the delivery room for the birth of ideas, a place where
history comes to life.
-Norman Cousins

If history repeats itself, and the unexpected always happens,
how incapable must man be of learning from experience.
-George Bernard Shaw

Study history, study history. In history lies all the secrets of
statecraft.
-Winston Churchill

To me history ought to be a source of pleasure. It isn't just part
of our civic responsibility. To me it's an enlargement of the
experience of being alive, just the way literature or art or music
is.
-David McCullough

History is a vast early warning system. -Norman Cousins

It is always better to imitate a successful man than to envy him.
-Napoleon Hill

Most of us spend too much time on the last twenty-four hours
and too little on the past six thousand years.
-Will Durant

No great man lives in vain. The history of the world is but the
biography of great men. -Thomas Carlyle

Men do not learn much from the lessons of history and that is
the most important of all the lessons of history.
-Aldous Huxley

*Rest, nature, books and music...such is my idea
of happiness.*
-Leo Tolstoy

Read-It maketh the full man.

*To be able to read and associate the
meaning with the words read.*

Not all readers are leaders, but all leaders are readers.
-Harry S. Truman

If you have a garden and a library, you have everything you need.
-Marcus Tullius Cicero

The person, be it gentleman or lady, who has not pleasure in a good novel, must be intolerably stupid.
-Jane Austen

The man who does not read has no advantage over the man who cannot read.
-Mark Twain

I believe that it is better to tell the truth than a lie. I believe it is better to be free than to be a slave. And I believe it is better to know than to be ignorant.
-H. L. Mencken

An investment in knowledge pays the best interest.
-Benjamin Franklin

Properly, we should read for power. Man reading should be man intensively alive. The book should be a ball of light in one's hand.
-Ezra Pound

147

John C. McHugh M.D.

You can tell a lot about a person by who his or her heroes are.
-Steve Jobs

If you want your children to be intelligent, read them fairy tales.
If you want them to be more intelligent, read them more fairy
tales.
-Albert Einstein

A man only learns in two ways, one by reading, and the other by
association with smarter people.
-Will Rogers

So, please, oh please, we beg, we pray, go throw your TV set
away, and in its place you can install, a lovely bookcase on the
wall.
-Roald Dahl

Some books leave us free and some books make us free.
-Ralph Waldo Emerson

If you want to earn more, learn more.
-Zig Ziglar

The love of learning, the sequestered nooks, And all the sweet
serenity of books.
-Henry Wadsworth Longfellow

I will defend the importance of bedtime stories to my last gasp.
-J. K. Rowling

Reading maketh a full man; conference a ready man; and writing
an exact man.
-Francis Bacon

There are three kinds of men. The one that learns by reading.
The few who learn by observation. The rest of them have to pee
on the electric fence for themselves.
-Will Rogers

Love of books is the best of all. -Jackie Kennedy

Books are those faithful mirrors that reflect to our mind the
minds of sages and heroes.
-Edward Gibbon

We shouldn't teach great books; we should teach a love of
reading. Knowing the contents of a few works of literature is a
trivial achievement. Being inclined to go on reading is a great
achievement.
-B. F. Skinner

If we encounter a man of rare intellect, we should ask him what
books he reads.
-Ralph Waldo Emerson

The mind, once stretched by a new idea, never returns to its
original dimensions.
-Ralph Waldo Emerson

A bookstore is one of the only pieces of evidence we have that
people are still thinking.
-Jerry Seinfeld

Read no history: nothing but biography, for that is life without
theory.
-Benjamin Disraeli

Wear the old coat and buy the new book.
-Austin Phelps

I would trade all of my technology for an afternoon with
Socrates.
-Steve Jobs

I say there is no darkness but ignorance.
-Shakespeare

Read about history, and you become aware that nothing starts
with us.
-James Mattis

Never underestimate your own ignorance.
-Albert Einstein

Education-It is only the start/Your foundation.

Someone once said that education is the process by which a set of principles are driven down your throat. Right now all of you are debating this for yourself in your own minds. Some pro and some con. You see we can all decide for ourselves. We have that option. To think, to consider and then to debate and arriving at a solution common to all.

I have never let my schooling interfere with my education.
-Mark Twain

Knowledge isn't power until it is applied.
-Dale Carnegie

Education: the path from cocky ignorance to miserable uncertainty.
-Mark Twain

Education is the kindling of a flame, not the filling of a vessel.
-Socrates

Everybody is ignorant, only on different subjects.
-Will Rogers

Education is what remains after one has forgotten what one has learned in school. -Albert Einstein

151

A thorough knowledge of the Bible is worth more than a college
education.
-Theodore Roosevelt

Judge a man by his questions rather than his answers.
-Voltaire

Formal education will make you a living; self-education will
make you a fortune.
-John Rohn

Training is everything. The peach was once a bitter almond;
cauliflower is nothing but cabbage with a college education.
-Mark Twain

My son stuffed six years of college into a four year degree.--
Anonymous

Does college pay? They do if you are a good open-field runner.
-Will Rogers

If you want to be successful, it's just this simple. Know what you
are doing. Love what you are doing. And believe in what you are
doing.
-Will Rogers

Everybody is ignorant, only on different subjects.
-Will Rogers

Actual combat experience is the only teacher. You never come
out of a skirmish without having picked up a couple of new
tricks; without having learned more about your enemy...Total
involvement with the war was the only thing that kept me alive
and pushing.
-Audie Murphy

I'd like to know why well-educated idiots keep apologizing for
lazy and complaining people who think the world owes them a
living.
-John Wayne

The value of a college education is not the learning of many facts
but the training of the mind to think.
-Albert Einstein

The beautiful thing about learning is nobody can take it away
from you.
-B. B. King

Soap and education are not as sudden as a massacre, but they are
more deadly in the long run.
-Mark Twain

Every man should have a college education in order to show him
how little the thing is really worth.
-Elbert Hubbard

The things taught in schools and colleges are not an education,
but the means to an education.
-Ralph Waldo Emerson

College isn't the place to go for ideas.
-Helen Keller

That's what college is for - getting as many bad decisions as
possible out of the way before you're forced into the real world. I
keep a checklist of 'em on the wall in my room.
-Jeph Jacques

I spent three days a week for 10 years educating myself in the
public library, and it's better than college.
-Ray Bradbury

Intellectual growth should commence at birth and cease only at
death.
-Albert Einstein

Education without values, as useful as it is, seems rather to make
man a more clever devil.
-C. S. Lewis

He who opens a school door, closes a prison.
-Victor Hugo

Education begins the gentleman, but reading, good company and
reflection must finish him.
-John Locke

Good manners will open doors that the best education cannot.
-Clarence Thomas

The foundation stones for a balanced success are honesty,
character, integrity, faith, love and loyalty.
-Zig Ziglar

The fool wonders, the wise man asks. -Benjamin Disraeli

One pound of learning requires ten pounds of common sense to
apply it.
-Persian Proverb

I would challenge you to a battle of wits, but I see you are
unarmed! -William Shakespeare

Thinking is hard work; that's why so few do it.
-Albert Einstein

The only person who is educated is the one who has learned
how to learn and change.
-Carl Rogers

The whole purpose of education is to turn mirrors into
windows.
-Sydney J. Harris

To acquire knowledge, one must study; but to acquire wisdom,
one must observe.
-Marilyn vos Savant

The only place success comes before work is in the dictionary.
-Vince Lombardi

Reduce your plan to writing. The moment you complete this, you will have definitely given concrete form to the intangible desire.
-Napoleon Hill

Plan: Fail to plan-Plan to fail.

> *"Where do we go from here?" That is what the band Chicago asked of you years back and that is what I am now asking.*

I f you don't know where you are going, you'll end up someplace else.
-Yogi Berra

Even if you're on the right track, you'll get run over if you just sit there.
-Will Rogers

Experience is not what happens to a man; it is what a man does with what happens to him.
-Adous Huxley

You don't have to be great at something to start, but you have to start to be great at something.
-Zig Ziglar

It is a paradoxical but profoundly true and important principle of life that the most likely way to reach a goal is to be aiming not at that goal itself but at some more ambitious goal beyond it.
-Arnold Toynbee

Make each day your masterpiece.
-John wooden

It's not the will to win that matters – everyone has that. It's the will to prepare to win that matters.
-Bear Bryant

Don't just live a life; build one. -Steve Jobs

By failing to prepare, you are preparing to fail.
-Benjamin Franklin

Give me six hours to chop down a tree and I will spend the first
four sharpening the axe.
-Abraham Lincoln

Life is what happens to you while you're busy making other
plans.
-John Lennon

Shallow men believe in luck. Strong men believe in cause and
effect.
-Ralph Waldo Emerson

The longest journey begins with a single step.
-Patanjali

If you aim at nothing, you will hit it every time.
-Zig Ziglar

The wise man bridges the gap by laying out the path by means of
which he can get from where he is to where he wants to go.
-J. P. Morgan

Let our advance worrying become advance thinking and
planning.
-Winston Churchill

Being busy does not always mean real work. The object of all
work is production or accomplishment and to either of these
ends there must be forethought, system, planning, intelligence,
and honest purpose, as well as perspiration. Seeming to do is not
doing. -Thomas A. Edison

There is no short cut to achievement. Life requires thorough
preparation - veneer isn't worth anything.
-George Washington Carver

It wasn't raining when Noah built the ark. -Howard Ruff

157

*If you don't like something, change it. If you
can't change it, change your attitude.
-Maya Angelou*

Change-Expect it Embrace It.

> *All of us are uniquely different and all of us have placed different values in different things. But there is one thing that is common to all of us at this particular moment in our lives. That is the will to embark on something new.*

T o improve is to change; to be perfect is to change often.
                    -Winston Churchill

Every woman that finally figured out her worth, has picked up her suitcases of pride and boarded a flight to freedom, which landed in the valley of change.
-Shannon L. Alder

The universe is change; our life is what our thoughts make it.
-Marcus Aurelius

Innovation is the ability to see change as an opportunity - not a threat. -Steve Jobs

Only the wisest and stupidest of men never change.
-Confucius

Our greatest ability as humans is not to change the world; but to change ourselves. -Mahatma Gandhi

It is a bad plan that cannot be altered. -Publilius Syrus

I cannot say whether things will get better if we change; what I can say is they must change if they are to get better.
-Georg C. Lichtenberg

The snake which cannot cast its skin has to die. As well the minds which are prevented from changing their opinions; they cease to be mind.
-Friedrich Nietzsche

It irritates me to be told how things have always been done. I defy the tyranny of precedent. I cannot afford the luxury of a closed mind.
-Clara Barton

There are three constants in life... change, choice and principles.
-Stephen Covey

Change is inevitable. Change is constant.
-Benjamin Disraeli

If you want to succeed you should strike out on new paths, rather than travel the worn paths of accepted success.
-John D. Rockefeller

Following the light of the sun, we left the Old World.
-Christopher Columbus

The man who is swimming against the stream knows the strength of it.
-Woodrow Wilson

The dogmas of the quiet past are inadequate to the stormy present. The occasion is piled high with difficulty, and we must rise with the occasion. As our case is new, we must think anew and act anew.
-Abraham Lincoln

It often takes more courage to change one's opinion than to stick to it. -Georg C. Lichtenberg

God grant me the serenity to accept the things I cannot change, the courage to change the things I can, and the wisdom to know the difference.
-Reinhold Niebuhr

*I don't think about all the misery but of the
beauty that remains.
-Anne Frank*

Positive Attitude-You are happy because you whistle.

> *Whether it is to pursue individual interests or college we have got to have the attitude to win. Never consider anything too difficult.*

T he first time you quit, it's hard. The second time, it gets easier. The third time, you don't even have to think about it.
-Bear Bryant

People often say that motivation doesn't last. Well, neither does bathing - that's why we recommend it daily.
-Zig Ziglar

Positive anything is better than negative nothing.
-Elbert Hubbard

Positive thinking will let you do everything better than negative thinking will.
-Zig Ziglar

Your attitude, not your aptitude, will determine your altitude.
-Zig Ziglar

They all laughed when I said I'd become a comedian. Well, they're not laughing now.
-Bob Monkhouse

They're not going to get me.
-John Dillinger

If you think you can do a thing or think you can't do a thing,
you're right.
-Henry ford

Fears are paper tigers.
-Amelia Earhart

When everything seems to be going against you, remember that
the airplane takes off against the wind, not with it.
-Henry Ford

Age wrinkles the body. Quitting wrinkles the soul.
-Douglas MacArthur

I will not let anyone walk through my mind with their dirty feet.
-Mahatma Gandhi

Hang on to your youthful enthusiasms - you'll be able to use
them better when you're older.
-Seneca

If they don't have a winning attitude, I don't want them.
-Bear Bryant

An angry man is again angry with himself when he returns to
reason.
-Publilius Syrus

A pessimist sees the difficulty in every opportunity; an optimist
sees the opportunity in every difficulty.
-Winston Churchill

Tall men come down to my height when I hit 'em in the body.
-Jack Dempsey

Let other pens dwell on guilt and misery.
-Jane Austen

The most important decision you make is to be in a good mood.
-Voltaire

163

There is always a light within us that is free from all sorrow and grief, no matter how much we may be experiencing suffering.
-Patanjali

To live is the rarest thing in the world. Most people exist, that is all.
-Oscar Wilde

I hear you're looking for a sexy blonde to play with the Marx Brothers. Would you like to see me? I'm blonde and I'm sexy.
-Marilyn Monroe

To all the girls that think you're fat because you're not a size zero, you're the beautiful one, its society who's ugly.
-Marilyn Monroe

The challenge of leadership is to be strong, but not rude; be kind, but not weak; be bold, but not a bully; be thoughtful, but not lazy; be humble, but not timid; be proud, but not arrogant; have humor, but without folly.
-John Rohn

You can make positive deposits in your own economy every day by reading and listening to powerful, positive, life-changing content and by associating with encouraging and hope-building people.
-Zig Ziglar

The only reason they come to see me is that I know that life is great, and they know I know it.
-Clark Gable

Weakness of attitude becomes weakness of character.
-Albert Einstein

The Wright brothers flew through the smoke screen of impossibility. -Dorothea Brande

It is not in the stars to hold our destiny but in ourselves.
-Shakespeare

Actions speak louder than words, and a smile says, 'I like you.
You make me happy. I am glad to see you."
-Dale Carnegie

Low self-esteem is like driving through life with the hand brakes
on.
-Maxwell Maltz

He who sings frightens away his ills.
-Miguel de Cervantes

I never blame myself when I'm not hitting. I just blame the bat
and if it keeps up, I change bats. After all, if I know it isn't my
fault that I'm not hitting, how can I get mad at myself?
-Yogi Berra

I don't lose any sleep at night over the potential for failure. I
cannot even spell the word.
-General James Mattis

There has never been a statue erected to honor a critic.
-Zig Ziglar

When God sends the dawn, he sends it for all.
-Miguel de Cervantes

Optimism doesn't wait on facts. It deals with prospects.
Pessimism is a waste of time.
-Norman Cousins

The best is yet to come.
-William Shakespeare

You make mistakes. Mistakes don't make you.
-Maxwell Maltz

Don't bring negative to my door.
-Maya Angelou

Nothing is impossible. -Walt Disney

*Tall men come down to my height when I hit
'em in the body.*
-Jack Dempsey

Confidence/Humor-Buckle In
with a Grin.

Who was it who said it couldn't be done
But he with a chuckle replied, "Maybe it
can't but I'll be one
Who won't say so until I've tried."
So he buckled right in with a bit of a grin
And if it hurt he didn't show it
He tackled the thing that couldn't be done
And he did it!

Oh Lord, thou givest us everything, at the price of an effort.
-Leonardo Da Vinci

Say not always what you know, but always know what you say.
-Claudius

It always seems impossible until it's done.
-Nelson Mandela

Most of the important things in the world have been accomplished by people who have kept on trying when there seemed to be no hope at all.
-Dale Carnegie

I hated every minute of training, but I said, 'Don't quit. Suffer now and live the rest of your life as a champion.'
-Muhammad Ali

Let me embrace thee, sour adversity, for wise men say it is the wisest course. -Shakespeare

There is little success where there is little laughter. -Andrew Carnegie

I always tried to turn every disaster into an opportunity. -John D. Rockefeller

If you have to ask how much it costs, you can't afford it. -J.P. Morgan

It ain't bragging if you can do it. -Dizzy Dean

In order to attain the impossible, one must attempt the absurd. -Miguel de Cervantes

Ten minutes of genuine belly laughter had an anesthetic effect and would give me at least two hours of pain-free sleep. -Norman Cousins

Call on God, but row away from the rocks. -Indian Proverb

Our doubts are traitors and make us lose the good we oft might win by fearing to attempt. -William Shakespeare

The best pitchers have a short term memory and a bullet proof confidence. -Greg Maddux

Common sense and a sense of humor are the same thing, moving at different speeds. A sense of humor is just common sense dancing. -William James

Optimism is the faith that leads to achievement. Nothing can be done without hope and confidence. -Helen Keller

I'd be conceited if I said I could, but I'd be lying if I said I couldn't. -Rocky Marciano

Success is not final, failure is not fatal: it is the
courage to continue that counts.
-Winston Churchill

Accept the Challenge-
Persistence

> *We have got to have this attitude a will to win.*
> *Never say die. Yea it is going to be tough. The*
> *reward of something well done is to have done*
> *it. You've done it now what are you going to do*
> *with it?*

No one knows what he can do till he tries.
-Publilius Syrus

In life, you'll have your back up against the wall many times. You might as well get used to it.
-Bear Bryant

If you look around at the people in show business today they are basically the people who didn't give up.
-Brent Spiner

Permanence, perseverance and persistence in spite of all obstacles, discouragements and impossibilities: It is this, that in all things distinguishes the strong soul from the weak.
-Thomas Carlyle

Fall seven times; get up eight.
-Japanese Proverb

Nothing in the world can take the place of persistence. Talent will not; nothing is more common than unsuccessful men with talent. Genius will not; unrewarded genius is almost a proverb.

Education will not; the world is full of educated derelicts.
Persistence and determination alone are omnipotent.
-Calvin Coolidge

You can't plow a field simply by turning it over in your mind.
-Gordon B. Hinckley

When you get into a tight place, and everything goes against you
till it seems as if you couldn't hold on a minute longer, never give
up then, for that's just the place and time that the tide will turn.
-Harriet Beecher Stowe

You only live once, but if you do it right, once is enough.
-Mae West

No; small timers get into it, and ruin it for everyone.
-John Dillinger

Life has no limitations, except the ones you make.
-Les Brown

Laughter is not at all a bad beginning for a friendship, and it is
far the best ending for one.
-Oscar Wilde

The purpose of life is to live it, to taste experience to the utmost,
to reach out eagerly and without fear for newer and richer
experience.
-Eleanor Roosevelt

The ideal man bears the accidents of life with dignity and grace,
making the best of circumstances.
-Aristotle

Without training, they lacked knowledge. Without knowledge,
they lacked confidence. Without confidence, they lacked
victory.
-Julius Caesar

The secret of success is constancy to purpose.
-Benjamin Disraeli

The flame that burns twice as bright burns half as long.
-Lao Tzu

Energy and persistence conquer all things.
-Benjamin Franklin

Success is not the absence of failure; it's the persistence through
failure.
-Aisha Tyler

Paralyze resistance with persistence.
-Woody Hayes

The three great essentials to achieve anything worthwhile are,
first, hard work; second, stick-to-itiveness; third, common sense.
-Thomas A. Edison

You just can't beat the person who never gives up.
-Babe Ruth

In the confrontation between the stream and the rock, the
stream always wins-not through strength, but through
persistence.
-Buddha

Courage and perseverance have a magical talisman, before which
difficulties disappear and obstacles vanish into air.
-John Quincy Adams

Let me tell you the secret that has led to my goal. My strength
lies solely in my tenacity. -Louis Pasteur

If your determination is fixed, I do not counsel you to despair.
Few things are impossible to diligence and skill. Great works are
performed not by strength, but perseverance.
-Samuel Johnson

The game's isn't over until it's over.
-Yogi Berra

Every man's got to figure to get beat sometime.
-Joe Louis

That which does not kill us makes us stronger.
-Friedrich Nietzsche

Our greatest glory is not in never falling, but in rising every time
we fall.
-Confucius

Don't stop when you're tired; stop when you're done.
-Marilyn Monroe

Strength does not come from winning. When you go through
hardships and decide not to surrender, that is strength.
-Mahatma Gandhi

Remember that failure is an event, not a person.
-Zig Ziglar

It does not matter how slowly you go as long as you do not stop.
-Confucius

Energy and persistence conquer all things.
-Benjamin Franklin

Studies indicate that the one quality all successful people have is
persistence. They're willing to spend more time accomplishing a
task and to persevere in the face of many difficult odds. There's a
very positive relationship between people's ability to accomplish
any task and the time they're willing to spend on it.
-Joyce Brothers

Failure is unimportant. It takes courage to make a fool of
yourself.
-Charlie Chaplin

John C. McHugh M.D.

Patience, persistence and perspiration make an unbeatable
combination for success.
-Napoleon Hill

Success consists of going from failure to failure without loss of
enthusiasm.
-Winston Churchill

It ain't over till it's over.
-Yogi Berra

I do not think that there is any other quality so essential to
success of any kind as the quality of perseverance. It overcomes
almost everything, even nature.
-John D .Rockefeller

Love and work are the only two real things in our lives. They
belong together, otherwise it is off. Work is in itself a form of
love.
-Marilyn Monroe

The slogan 'press on' has solved and always will solve the
problems of the human race.
-Calvin Coolidge

When deeds speak, words are nothing.
-African Proverb

People always say I didn't give up my seat because I was tired,
but that isn't true...No, the only tired I was, was tired of giving
in.
-Rosa Parks

It's not that I'm so smart, it's just that I stay with problems
longer.
-Albert Einstein

If you can't fly then run, if you can't run then walk, if you can't
walk then crawl, but whatever you do you have to keep moving
forward. -Martin Luther King, Jr.

Temper is what gets most of us into trouble.
Pride is what keeps us there.
-Mark Twain

Pride-The good and the bad kind-Understand the difference.

> That concludes my speech but there is something I feel compelled to say and there isn't but one way to say it.
> In my four years of attending LaGrange Senior High...
> **I was damn proud to be a Granger!**
> June 1, 1973
> John McHugh
> Graduation Commencement

I'd like to thank the good Lord for making me a Yankee.

-Joe Dimaggio

If you believe in yourself and have dedication and pride-and never quit-you'll be a winner. The price of victory is high but so are the rewards.
-Bear Bryant

Neither praise nor blame yourself.
-American Proverb

There are two kinds of pride, both good and bad. 'Good pride' represents our dignity and self-respect. 'Bad pride' is the deadly sin of superiority that reeks of conceit and arrogance.
-John C. Maxwell

We are rarely proud when we are alone. -Voltaire

Generosity is giving more than you can, and pride is taking less
than you need.
-Kahlil Gibran

All men make mistakes, but a good man yields when he knows
his course is wrong, and repairs the evil. The only crime is pride.
-Sophocles

Pride is the only poison you can swallow that won't kill you.
-Anonymous

Proud people breed sad sorrows for themselves.
-Emily Brontë

Pride goes before destruction, a haughty spirit before a fall.
-Proverbs 16:18

It was pride that changed angels into devils; it is humility that
makes men as angels. -Saint Augustine

A proud man is always looking down on things and people; and,
of course, as long as you are looking down, you cannot see
something that is above you.
-C.S. Lewis

Through pride we are ever deceiving ourselves. But deep down
below the surface of the average conscience a still, small voice
says to us, something is out of tune.
-C.G. Jung

Put away your pride and put on humble clothes. -Rumi
Pride costs us more than hunger, thirst, and cold.
-Thomas Jefferson

Talent is God given. Be humble. Fame is man-given. Be grateful.
Conceit is self-given. Be careful.
-John Wooden

The more pride we have the more other people's pride irritates
us. -C.S. Lewis

177

Pride is both a virtue and a vice.
-Theodore Parker

Lord Bacon told Sir Edward Coke when he was boasting, The less you speak of your greatness, the more shall I think of it.
-William Shakespeare

God opposes the proud, but gives grace to the humble.
-James 4:6

Pride helps us; and pride is not a bad thing when it only urges us to hide our own hurts, not to hurt others.
-George Eliot

Pride sullies the noblest character.
-Claudius

Show class, have pride and display character. If you do winning will take care of itself.
-Bear Bryant

It's a fine thing to rise above pride, but you must have pride in order to do so.
-Georges Bernanos

Humility and knowledge in poor clothes excel pride and ignorance in costly attire.
-William Penn

My pride fell with my fortunes.
-William Shakespeare

Be nice to people on your way up because you're gonna meet them on your way down.
-Jimmy Durante

Human pride is not worthwhile; there is always something lying in wait to take the wind out of it.
-Mark Twain

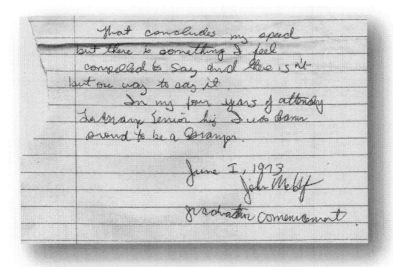

"That concludes my speech but there is something I feel
compelled to say and there isn't but one way to say it.
In my four years of attending LaGrange Senior High...

I was damn proud to be a Granger!

June 1, 1973
John McHugh
Graduation Commencement

John C. McHugh M.D.

Epilogue

You got to be to do and you got to do to have.
-Zig Ziglar

So you've graduated from high school, college, or graduate
school; now what are you going to do? I chose to pursue
medicine; what are your plans? How will you achieve them?
Let's break it down.

You got to be: This is who you are and you can control this.

- Espouse to embody the virtues and qualities mentioned
  in this book. Note that historical, famous, and successful
  people who have come before you deemed them
  important.
- You've got to be a good person, demonstrate integrity,
  and give back. Another favorite Ziglar quote you'll find
  useful is, "You'll get what you want in life if you help
  enough people get what they want."
- Do as Lou Holtz admonished his National
  Championship football team at Notre Dame to do: "I
  follow three rules: Do the right thing, do the best you
  can, and always show people you care."
- I believe that the quote sometimes attributed to Woody
  Allen speaks volumes and is a baseline rule to live by:
  "80% of success is just showing up."
- You have to continually work to be a better version of
  yourself. Read, read, and then read. There is no better
  place to start than reading biographies of famous and
  successful people. (I listen to books when I walk.)

- Listen to your mentors remembering that, "A smart person learns from experience and a wise one from advice."

You got to do: You have your degree but you have no experience.

- When I had finally finished college, medical school, and then completed my residency thirteen years after high school, what did I have? Well...I had a MD after my name, but I had very little practical experience, I had no reputation of being good at urology, and I had no patients. Regardless of your planned endeavors, you are going to need to gain experience and hone your skills. You will have to...do!

- To do what you are going to do well, you will need to have and heed the virtues and characteristics mentioned in this book.

- Self-help books provide a purpose in that they put into writing something you might have felt or noticed and make it comprehendible. (*The 7 Habits of Highly Successful People* by Stephen Covey is my favorite.) My little brother Jeff is in sales and years ago he gave me several Zig Ziglar cassette tapes. I loved them and learned so much about people and the importance of a positive attitude. I also noted that the characteristics needed to succeed in sales are not that much different than succeeding in medicine. The quote, "The physician should have a ready wit as a dour disposition is repulsive to the well and sick alike" works for any profession. You market yourself by being positive. "Don't advertise your problems, there's not a market for them." Ziglar said that you needed to listen to or read motivational writings daily and "I take a shower twice a day to get the world's dirt off me, so too I need to read positive things daily to get rid of the world's negativity."

- I think as you read about famous people and learn about their path to achievement you'll find one quality repeatedly cropping up and that is perseverance. As

Churchill said to Britain in World War II, "Never, never, never give up," and of course my favorite, "It's hard to beat a man who won't quit."

- We talk of pride being both a virtue and a vice, but when it comes to doing a good job, it is important to take pride in your work knowing you did the best you could do. Someone else may not know, but you'll know.

To have: Having things comes with time and it is earned, but it doesn't stop there.

- Everybody wants to have a soul mate, a nice house, a dependable car, and enough money in the bank to be comfortable. This is the "having" part. These things don't just happen; having the things you want is a result of who you are and what you have done with your potential. Having is built upon the "To be" and the "To do" part of you.
- Two entry level sales people are given the same company support, the same type of territory to work, and the same product to sell. However, one does extremely better than the other, why is that? You need to be the person who gets to work first, stays later than the rest, makes more cold calls, sees more prospective clients, and has a follow up strategy. My brother Jeff tells me that it is easy to review a sales associates' activity log to assess the reason their performance is doing well or not. "It's a numbers game John. The more calls you make and the more people you talk to, the better you do."
- Once you have the "have", you then must continually build on your success by "being" a person of integrity and "doing" what is required of you. It becomes a repeating cycle with each attribute necessary for the next. Life is dynamic and each new revolution of this cycle should be an improvement over the last.
- Although the goal of a career is to be successful, having things is meaningless if you are not happy with yourself, your home life, and family. This is where being the person you know you should be balances the non-business aspects of your life so things work in unison.

People Quoted

A ll of the pictures and people who are quoted are for one reason or another, famous, successful, and have contributed to humanity. An easy thing to do is to read about these people and rather than blaze a trail of your own learn from their experiences. Their stories will not only instruct but will inspire you. You will note that not much has changed in the human condition of today when compared to time of Confucius, Aristotle, Caesar and Shakespeare.

Kareem Abdul-Jabbar is an American retired professional basketball player who played 20 seasons in the National Basketball Association for the Milwaukee Bucks and the Los Angeles Lakers. Wikipedia
Born: April 16, 1947, New York City, NY

John Quincy Adams was an American statesman who served as a diplomat, minister and ambassador to foreign nations, and treaty negotiator, United States Senator, U.S. Representative from Massachusetts. Wikipedia
Born: July 11, 1767, Braintree, MA
Died: February 23, 1848, Washington, D.C.

Aesop was a Greek fabulist and story teller credited with a number of fables now collectively known as Aesop's Fables. Wikipedia
Born: 600 BC, Amorium
Died: 564 BC, Delphi, Greece

Shannon L. Alder is an inspirational author. Her tidbits of wisdom have been published in over 100 different books by various relationship authors and in several online magazine articles.

Maya Angelou was an American poet, memoirist, and civil rights activist. She published seven autobiographies, three books of essays, several books of poetry, and was credited with a list of plays, movies, and television shows spanning over 50 years. Wikipedia
Born: April 4, 1928, St. Louis, MO
Died: May 28, 2014, Winston-Salem, NC

John C. McHugh M.D.

Muhammad Ali was an American professional boxer and activist. He is widely regarded as one of the most significant and celebrated sports figures of the 20th century. Wikipedia
Born: January 17, 1942, Louisville, KY
Died: June 3, 2016, Scottsdale, AZ

Aristotle was an ancient Greek philosopher and scientist born in the city of Stagira, Chalkidice, on the northern periphery of Classical Greece. Wikipedia
Born: 384 BC, Stagira
Died: 322 BC, Chalcis, Greece

Margaret Eleanor Atwood is a Canadian poet, novelist, literary critic, essayist, inventor, and environmental activist. Wikipedia
Born: November 18, 1939, Ottawa, Canada
Poems: Morning in the Burned House, MORE
Movies: The Handmaid's Tale.

Augustine of Hippo was an early Roman African Christian theologian and philosopher from the Roman province of Africa whose writings influenced the development of Western Christianity and Western philosophy. Wikipedia
Born: November 13, 354 AD, Thagaste
Died: August 28, 430 AD, Hippo Regius, Algeria

Augustus was the founder of the Roman Principate and considered the first Roman emperor, controlling the Roman Empire from 27 BC until his death in AD 14. Wikipedia
Born: 63 BC, Ancient Rome
Died: August 19, 14 AD, Nola, Italy

Marcus Aurelius was Roman emperor from 161 to 180, ruling jointly with Lucius Verus until Verus' death in 169 and jointly with his son, Commodus, from 177. He was the last of the so-called Five Good Emperors. Wikipedia
Born: April 26, 121 AD, Rome, Italy
Died: March 17, 180 AD, Vindobona, Austria

Jane Austen was an English novelist known primarily for her six major novels, which interpret, critique and comment upon the British landed gentry at the end of the 18th century. Wikipedia
Born: December 16, 1775, Steventon, United Kingdom
Died: July 18, 1817, Winchester, United Kingdom

Francis Bacon, 1st Viscount, was an English philosopher, statesman, scientist, jurist, orator, and author. He served both as Attorney General and as Lord Chancellor of England. Wikipedia
Born: January 22, 1561, Strand, London, United Kingdom
Died: April 9, 1626, Highgate, United Kingdom

Joseph Louis Barrow, best known as Joe Louis and nicknamed the "Brown Bomber", was an American professional boxer who competed from 1934 to 1951. Wikipedia
Born: May 13, 1914, La Fayette, AL
Died: April 12, 1981, Paradise, NV

Clarissa "Clara" Harlowe Barton was a pioneering nurse who founded the American Red Cross. She was a hospital nurse in the American Civil War, a teacher, and patent clerk. Wikipedia
Born: December 25, 1821, Oxford
Died: April 12, 1912, Glen Echo, MD

Melody Beattie is an American author of self-help books on codependent relationships. Wikipedia
Born: 1948, Saint Paul, MN

Henry Ward Beecher was an American Congregationalist clergyman, social reformer, and speaker, known for his support of the abolition of slavery, his emphasis on God's love, and his 1875 adultery trial. Wikipedia
Born: June 24, 1813, Litchfield, CT
Died: March 8, 1887, Brooklyn, New York City, NY

Geneviève Behrend was a French-born author and teacher of Mental Science, a New Thought discipline created by Thomas Troward. There is little known about her early life except that one of her parents was Scottish. Wikipedia
Born: 1881, Paris, France
Died: 1960, United States of America

Louis Émile Clément Georges Bernanos was a French author, and a soldier in World War I. A Roman Catholic with monarchist leanings, he was critical of bourgeois thought and was opposed to what he identified as defeatism. Wikipedia
Born: February 20, 1888, Paris, France
Died: July 5, 1948, Neuilly-sur-Seine, France

John C. McHugh M.D.

Lawrence Peter "Yogi" Berra was an American professional baseball catcher, who later took on the roles of manager, and coach. He played 19 seasons in Major League Baseball, all but the last for the New York Yankees. Wikipedia
Born: May 12, 1925, The Hill, St. Louis, MO
Died: September 22, 2015, West Caldwell, NJ

Jeffrey Preston Bezos is an American technology and retail entrepreneur, investor, electrical engineer, computer scientist, and philanthropist, best known as the founder, chairman, and chief executive of Amazon. Wikipedia
Spouse: MacKenzie Bezos (m. 1993) Trending
Born: January 12, 1964, Albuquerque, NM

Josh Billings was the pen name of 19th-century American humorist Henry Wheeler Shaw. He was a famous humor writer and lecturer in the United States, perhaps second only to Mark Twain, during the latter half of the 19th century. Wikipedia
Born: April 21, 1818, Lanesborough, MA
Died: October 14, 1885, Monterey, CA

Dietrich Bonhoeffer was a German pastor, theologian, spy, anti-Nazi dissident, and key founding member of the Confessing Church. Wikipedia
Born: February 4, 1906, Wrocław, Poland
Died: April 9, 1945, Flossenbürg concentration camp, Germany

Neal A Boortz, Jr. is an American author, attorney, and former Libertarian radio host. His nationally syndicated talk show, The Neal Boortz Show, which ended in 2013, was carried throughout the United States. Wikipedia
Born: April 6, 1945 (age 72), Bryn Mawr, Lower Merion Township, PA

Ray Douglas Bradbury was an American author and screenwriter. He worked in a variety of genres, including fantasy, science fiction, horror, and mystery fiction. Wikipedia
Born: August 22, 1920, Waukegan, IL
Died: June 5, 2012, Los Angeles, CA

Dorothea Brande was a writer and editor in New York. She was born in Chicago and attended the University of Chicago, the Lewis Institute in Chicago, and the University of Michigan. Wikipedia
Born: 1893, United States of America

Died: 1948, New Hampshire

Sarah Ban Breathnach, is a best-selling author, philanthropist and public speaker. She is the author of thirteen books, including Simple Abundance: A Daybook of Comfort and Joy. Wikipedia
Born: May 5, 1947, Westbury, NY

Emily Jane Brontë was an English novelist and poet who is best known for her only novel, Wuthering Heights, now considered a classic of English literature. Wikipedia
Born: July 30, 1818, Thornton, West Yorkshire, United Kingdom
Died: December 19, 1848, Haworth, United Kingdom

Joyce Diane Brothers was an American psychologist, television personality and columnist, who wrote a daily newspaper advice column from 1960 to 2013. Wikipedia
Born: October 20, 1927, Brooklyn, New York City, NY
Died: May 13, 2013, Fort Lee, NJ

Harriett Jackson Brown Jr. is an American author best known for his inspirational book, Life's Little Instruction Book, which was a New York Times bestseller. Wikipedia
Born: 1940, Middle Tennessee

Leslie Calvin "Les" Brown is an American motivational speaker, author, radio DJ, former television host, and former politician. As a politician, he is a former member of the Ohio House of Representatives. Wikipedia
Born: February 17, 1945, Liberty City, Miami, FL

Paul William "Bear" Bryant was an American college football player and coach. He was best known as the longtime head coach of the University of Alabama football team. Wikipedia
Born: September 11, 1913, Cleveland County, Arkansas, AR
Died: January 26, 1983, Tuscaloosa, AL

Gautama Buddha, also known as Siddhārtha Gautama, Shakyamuni Buddha, or simply the Buddha, after the title of Buddha, was an ascetic and sage, on whose teachings Buddhism was founded. Wikipedia
Born: Lumbini, Nepal
Died: Kushinagar, India

John C. McHugh M.D.

Dan Buettner is a National Geographic Fellow and New York Times bestselling author. He is an explorer, educator, author, producer, storyteller and public speaker. Wikipedia
Born: 1960, Saint Paul, Minnesota

Warren Edward Buffett is an American business magnate, investor, and philanthropist. Buffett serves as the chairman and CEO of Berkshire Hathaway. Wikipedia
Born: August 30, 1930, Omaha, NE

Carol Creighton Burnett is an American actress, comedian, singer and writer, whose career spans six decades of television. She is best known for her long-running TV variety show, The Carol Burnett Show, originally aired on CBS. Wikipedia
Born: April 26, 1933 (age 84), San Antonio, TX

Gaius Julius Caesar, usually called Julius Caesar, was a Roman politician and general who played a critical role in the events that led to the demise of the Roman Republic and the rise of the Roman Empire. Wikipedia
Born: July 13, 100 BC, Rome, Italy
Full name: Gaius Julius Caesar
Assassinated: March 15, 44 BC, Rome, Italy

Thomas Carlyle was a Scottish philosopher, satirical writer, essayist, translator, historian, mathematician, and teacher. Wikipedia
Born: December 4, 1795, Ecclefechan, United Kingdom
Died: February 5, 1881, London, United Kingdom

Andrew Carnegie was a Scottish-American industrialist, business magnate, and philanthropist. Carnegie led the expansion of the American steel industry in the late 19th century and is often identified as one of the richest people. Wikipedia
Born: November 25, 1835, Dunfermline, United Kingdom
Died: August 11, 1919, Lenox, MA

Dale Harbison Carnegie was an American writer and lecturer and the developer of famous courses in self-improvement, salesmanship, corporate training, public speaking, and interpersonal skills. Wikipedia
Born: November 24, 1888, Maryville, MO
Died: November 1, 1955, Forest Hills, New York City, NY

George Washington Carver was an American botanist and inventor. He became well-known to the public due to his active promotion of alternative crops to cotton and methods to prevent soil depletion. Wikipedia
Born: Diamond, MO
Died: January 5, 1943, Tuskegee, AL

Miguel de Cervantes was a Spanish writer who is widely regarded as the greatest writer in the Spanish language and one of the world's pre-eminent novelists. Wikipedia
Born: September 29, 1547, Alcalá de Henares, Spain
Died: April 22, 1616, Madrid, Spain

Gabrielle Bonheur "Coco" Chanel was a French fashion designer and businesswoman. She was the founder and namesake of the Chanel brand. Wikipedia
Born: August 19, 1883, Saumur, France
Died: January 10, 1971, Hôtel Ritz Paris, Paris, France

Sir Charles Spencer Chaplin, was an English comic actor, filmmaker, and composer who rose to fame in the era of silent film. Wikipedia
Born: April 16, 1889, Walworth, London, United Kingdom
Died: December 25, 1977, Corsier-sur-Vevey, Switzerland

Sir Winston Leonard Spencer-Churchill was a British statesman, army officer, and writer, who served as Prime Minister of the United Kingdom from 1940 to 1945 and again from 1951 to 1955. Wikipedia
Spouse: Clementine Churchill (m. 1908–1965) Trending
Born: November 30, 1874, Blenheim Palace, United Kingdom
Died: January 24, 1965, Kensington, London, United Kingdom

Marcus Tullius Cicero was a Roman politician and lawyer, who served as consul in the year 63 BC. He came from a wealthy municipal family of the Roman equestrian order, and is considered one of Rome's greatest orators and prose stylists. Wikipedia
Born: January 3, 106 BC, Arpino, Italy

Claudius was Roman emperor from 41 to 54. A member of the Julio-Claudian dynasty, he was the son of Drusus and Antonia Minor. He was born at Lugdunum in Gaul, the first Roman Emperor to be born outside Italy. Wikipedia
Born: August 1, 10 BC, Lugdunum

John C. McHugh M.D.

Died: October 13, 54 AD, Rome, Italy

Tyrus Raymond Cobb, nicknamed The Georgia Peach, was an
American Major League Baseball outfielder. He was born in rural
Narrows, Georgia. Wikipedia
Born: December 18, 1886, Narrows, GA
Died: July 17, 1961, Atlanta, GA

Robert Collier was an American author of self-help and New
Thought metaphysical books in the 20th century. He was the
nephew of Peter Fenelon Collier, founder of Collier's
Weekly. Wikipedia
Born: April 19, 1885, St. Louis, MO
Died: 1950, United States of America

Confucius was a Chinese teacher, editor, politician, and
philosopher of the Spring and Autumn period of Chinese
history. Wikipedia
Born: September 28, 551 BC
Died: 479 BC

Grace Anna Goodhue Coolidge was the wife of the 30th President
of the United States, Calvin Coolidge. She was the First Lady from
1923 to 1929. Wikipedia
Born: January 3, 1879, Burlington, VT
Died: July 8, 1957, Northampton, MA

John Calvin Coolidge Jr. was the 30th President of the United
States. A Republican lawyer from Vermont, Coolidge worked his
way up the ladder of Massachusetts state politics, eventually
becoming governor of that state. Wikipedia
Born: July 4, 1872, Plymouth Notch, Vermont, VT
Died: January 5, 1933, Northampton, MA

Norman Cousins was an American political journalist, author,
professor, and world peace advocate. Wikipedia
Born: June 24, 1915, Union City, NJ
Died: November 30, 1990, Los Angeles, CA
Awards: Albert Schweitzer Prize for Humanitarianism, Helmerich
Award

Stephen Richards Covey was an American educator, author,
businessman, and keynote speaker. His most popular book is The 7
Habits of Highly Effective People. Wikipedia

Born: October 24, 1932, Salt Lake City, UT
Died: July 16, 2012, Idaho Falls, ID

Roald Dahl was a British novelist, short story writer, poet,
screenwriter, and fighter pilot. His books have sold more than 250
million copies worldwide. Wikipedia
Born: September 13, 1916, Llandaff, Cardiff, United Kingdom
Died: November 23, 1990, Oxford, United Kingdom

Leonardo di ser Piero da Vinci, more commonly Leonardo da Vinci
or simply Leonardo, was an Italian Renaissance polymath whose
areas of interest included invention, painting, sculpting,
architecture, ... Wikipedia
Born: April 15, 1452, Anchiano, Italy
Died: May 2, 1519, Clos Lucé, Amboise, France

Jay Hanna "Dizzy" Dean, also known as Jerome Herman Dean, was
an American professional baseball player. He played in Major
League Baseball as a pitcher for the St. Louis Cardinals, Chicago
Cubs and the St. Louis Browns. Wikipedia
Born: January 16, 1910, Lucas, AR
Died: July 17, 1974, Reno, NV

William Harrison "Jack" Dempsey, nicknamed "Kid Blackie" and
"The Manassa Mauler", was an American professional boxer who
competed from 1914 to 1927, and reigned as the world heavyweight
champion from 1919 to 1926. Wikipedia
Born: June 24, 1895, Manassa, CO
Died: May 31, 1983, New York City, NY

John Herbert Dillinger was an American gangster in the
Depression-era United States. He operated with a group of men
known as the Dillinger Gang or Terror Gang, which was accused of
robbing 24 banks and four police stations, among other
activities. Wikipedia
Born: June 22, 1903, Indianapolis, IN
Died: July 22, 1934, Chicago, IL

Joseph Paul DiMaggio, nicknamed "Joltin' Joe" and "The Yankee
Clipper", was an American baseball center fielder who played his
entire 13-year career in Major League Baseball for the New York
Yankees. Wikipedia
Born: November 25, 1914, Martinez, CA
Died: March 8, 1999, Hollywood, FL

John C. McHugh M.D.

Benjamin Disraeli, 1st Earl of Beaconsfield, KG, PC, FRS was a British statesman of the Conservative Party who twice served as Prime Minister of the United Kingdom. Wikipedia
Born: December 21, 1804, Bloomsbury, London, United Kingdom
Died: April 19, 1881, Mayfair, London, United Kingdom

Frederick Douglass was an African-American social reformer, abolitionist, orator, writer, and statesman. Wikipedia
Born: Talbot County, MD
Died: February 20, 1895, Washington, D.C.

Peter Ferdinand Drucker was an Austrian-born American management consultant, educator, and author, whose writings contributed to the philosophical and practical foundations of the modern business corporation. Wikipedia
Born: November 19, 1909, Vienna, Austria
Died: November 11, 2005, Claremont, CA

John Dryden was an English poet, literary critic, translator, and playwright who was made England's first Poet Laureate in 1668. Wikipedia
Born: August 9, 1631, Aldwincle
Died: May 12, 1700, London, United Kingdom

William James "Will" Durant was an American writer, historian, and philosopher. He is best known for The Story of Civilization, 11 volumes written in collaboration with his wife, Ariel Durant, and published between 1935 and 1975. Wikipedia
Born: November 5, 1885, North Adams, MA
Died: November 7, 1981, United States of America

James Francis Durante was an American singer, pianist, comedian, and actor. His distinctive clipped gravelly speech, New York accent, comic language-butchery, jazz-influenced songs, and prominent nose. Wikipedia
Born: February 10, 1893, Manhattan, New York City, NY
Died: January 29, 1980, Santa Monica, CA

Wayne Walter Dyer was an American philosopher, self-help author, and a motivational speaker. His first book, Your Erroneous Zones, is one of the best-selling books of all time, with an estimated 35 million copies sold to date. Wikipedia
Born: May 10, 1940, Detroit, MI
Died: August 29, 2015, Maui County, Hawaii, HI

Amelia Mary Earhart was an American aviation pioneer and author. Earhart was the first female aviator to fly solo across the Atlantic Ocean. She received the U.S. Distinguished Flying Cross for this accomplishment. Wikipedia
Born: July 24, 1897, Atchison, KS

Thomas Alva Edison was an American inventor and businessman, who has been described as America's greatest inventor. Wikipedia
Born: February 11, 1847, Milan, OH
Died: October 18, 1931, Llewellyn Park, NJ

Albert Einstein was a German-born theoretical physicist who developed the theory of relativity, one of the two pillars of modern physics. Einstein's work is also known for its influence on the philosophy of science. Wikipedia
Born: March 14, 1879, Ulm, Germany
Died: April 18, 1955, Princeton, NJ

George Eliot (Mary Anne Evans) known by her pen name George Eliot, was an English novelist, poet, journalist, translator and one of the leading writers of the Victorian era. Wikipedia
Born: November 22, 1819, Nuneaton, United Kingdom
Died: December 22, 1880, Chelsea, London, United Kingdom

Ralph Waldo Emerson was an American essayist, lecturer, and poet who led the transcendentalist movement of the mid-19th century. Wikipedia
Born: May 25, 1803, Boston, MA
Died: April 27, 1882, Concord, MA
Poems: Brahma, The Rhodora, Boston Hymn, Concord Hymn, Terminus, Uriel
Education: Boston Latin School, Harvard Divinity School, Harvard University, Harvard College

Eminem (Marshall Bruce Mathers III) known professionally as Eminem, is an American rapper, songwriter, record producer, and actor. Eminem is the best-selling artist of the 2000s in the United States. Wikipedia
Born: October 17, 1972, Saint Joseph, MO

Epictetus was a Greek Stoic philosopher. He was born a slave at Hierapolis, Phrygia and lived in Rome until his banishment, when he went to Nicopolis in northwestern Greece for the rest of his life. Wikipedia

John C. McHugh M.D.

Born: 50 AD, Hierapolis, Turkey
Died: 135 AD, Nicopolis, Greece
Influenced: Marcus Aurelius, Arrian, Albert Ellis, James
Stockdale, Junius Rusticus, Han Ryner
Influenced by: Socrates, Zeno of
Citium, Diogenes, Chrysippus, Gaius Musonius Rufus, Hippocrates

Erasmus, known as Erasmus or Erasmus of Rotterdam, was a
Dutch Renaissance humanist, Catholic priest, social critic, teacher,
and theologian. Erasmus was a classical scholar and wrote in a
pure Latin style. Wikipedia
Born: October 1466, Rotterdam, Netherlands
Died: July 12, 1536, Basel, Switzerland

Cara Carleton "Carly" Fiorina is an American businessperson and
political figure, known primarily for her tenure as CEO of Hewlett-
Packard. She subsequently served as Chair of the philanthropic
organization Good360. Wikipedia
Born: September 6, 1954 (age 63), Austin, TX
Net worth: $59 million (2015)

Ella Jane Fitzgerald was an American jazz singer often referred to
as the First Lady of Song, Queen of Jazz, and Lady Ella. Wikipedia
Born: April 25, 1917, Newport News, VA
Died: June 15, 1996, Beverly Hills, CA

Malcolm Stevenson Forbes was an American entrepreneur most
prominently known as the publisher of Forbes magazine, founded
by his father B. C. Forbes. Wikipedia
Born: August 19, 1919, Brooklyn, New York City, NY
Died: February 24, 1990, Far Hills, NJ

Henry Ford was an American captain of industry and a business
magnate, the founder of the Ford Motor Company, and the sponsor
of the development of the assembly line technique of mass
production. Wikipedia
Born: July 30, 1863, Greenfield Township, Michigan
Died: April 7, 1947, Fair Lane, Dearborn, MI
Education: Detroit Business Institute

Annelies Marie "Anne" Frank was a German-born diarist. One of
the most discussed Jewish victims of the Holocaust, she gained
fame posthumously with the publication of The Diary of a Young
Girl. Wikipedia

Born: June 12, 1929, Frankfurt, Germany
Died: March 12, 1945, Bergen-Belsen concentration camp, Germany

Benjamin Franklin was a renowned polymath and one of the
Founding Fathers of the United States. Wikipedia
Born: January 17, 1706, Boston, MA
Died: April 17, 1790, Philadelphia, PA

William Clark Gable was an American film actor and military
officer, often referred to as "The King of Hollywood" or just simply
as "The King". Wikipedia
Born: February 1, 1901, Cadiz, OH
Died: November 16, 1960, Los Angeles, CA

Indira Priyadarshini Gandhi was an Indian stateswoman and
central figure of the Indian National Congress. She was the first
and, to date, the only female Prime Minister of India. Wikipedia
Born: November 19, 1917, Allahabad, India
Assassinated: October 31, 1984, New Delhi, India

Mahātmā Mohandas Karamchand Gandhi was an Indian activist
who was the leader of the Indian independence movement against
British rule. Wikipedia
Born: October 2, 1869, Porbandar, India
Assassinated: January 30, 1948, New Delhi, India

Marcus Mosiah Garvey Jr., was a proponent of Black nationalism
in Jamaica and especially the United States. Wikipedia
Born: August 17, 1887, Saint Ann's Bay, Jamaica
Died: June 10, 1940, West Kensington, United Kingdom

William Henry Gates III is an American business magnate,
investor, author, philanthropist, humanitarian and co-founder of
the Microsoft Corporation along with Paul Allen. Wikipedia
Born: October 28, 1955, Seattle, WA

Edward Gibbon was an English historian, writer and Member of
Parliament. His most important work, The History of the Decline
and Fall of the Roman Empire, was published in six volumes.
Wikipedia
Born: May 8, 1737, Putney, London, United Kingdom
Died: January 16, 1794, London, United Kingdom

John C. McHugh M.D.

Khalil Gibran was a Lebanese writer, poet and visual artist. Gibran was born in the town of Bsharri in the Mount Lebanon Mutasarrifate, Ottoman Empire (modern day Lebanon), to Khalil Gibran and Kamila Gibran (Rahmeh). Wikipedia
Born: January 6, 1883, Bsharri, Lebanon
Died: April 10, 1931, Saint Vincent's Catholic Medical Center, New York City, NY

Sir William Schwenck Gilbert was an English dramatist, librettist, poet and illustrator best known for the fourteen comic operas produced in collaboration with the composer Arthur Sullivan. Wikipedia
Born: November 18, 1836, Southampton Street, London, United Kingdom
Died: May 29, 1911, Harrow, London, United Kingdom

Johann Wolfgang von Goethe was a German writer and statesman. His works include epic and lyric poetry; prose and verse dramas; memoirs; an autobiography; literary and aesthetic criticism; treatises on botany, anatomy, and colour; and four novels. Wikipedia
Born: August 28, 1749, Goethe House, Frankfurt, Germany
Died: March 22, 1832, Weimar, Germany

Sir James Michael Goldsmith, a member of the prominent Goldsmith family, was an Anglo-French financier, tycoon and politician. In 1994 he was elected to represent a French constituency as a Member of the European Parliament. Wikipedia
Born: February 26, 1933, Paris, France
Died: July 18, 1997, Benahavís, Spain

Samuel Goldwyn, also known as Samuel Goldfish, was a Polish American film producer of Jewish descent. He was most well known for being the founding contributor and executive of several motion picture studios in Hollywood. Wikipedia
Born: August 17, 1879, Warsaw, Poland
Died: January 31, 1974, Los Angeles, CA

Nadine Gordimer was a South African writer, political activist and recipient of the 1991 Nobel Prize in Literature. Wikipedia
Born: November 20, 1923, Springs, South Africa
Died: July 13, 2014, Johannesburg, South Africa

Horace Greeley was founder and editor of the New-York Tribune, among the great newspapers of its time. Wikipedia
Born: February 3, 1811, Amherst, NH
Died: November 29, 1872, Pleasantville, NY

Sydney J. Harris was an American journalist for the Chicago Daily News and, later, the Chicago Sun-Times. Wikipedia
Born: September 14, 1917, London, United Kingdom
Died: December 8, 1986, Chicago, IL

Nathaniel Hawthorne was an American novelist, dark romantic, and short story writer. He was born in 1804 in Salem, Massachusetts to Nathaniel Hawthorne and the former Elizabeth Clarke Manning. Wikipedia
Born: July 4, 1804, Salem
Died: May 19, 1864, Plymouth, NH

Wayne Woodrow "Woody" Hayes was an American football player and coach. He served as the head coach at Denison University, Miami University in Oxford, Ohio, and Ohio State University. Wikipedia
Born: February 14, 1913, Clifton, OH
Died: March 12, 1987, Upper Arlington, OH

Ernest Miller Hemingway was an American novelist, short story writer, and journalist. His economical and understated style had a strong influence on 20th-century fiction, while his life of adventure and his public image influenced later generations. Wikipedia
Born: July 21, 1899, Oak Park, IL
Died: July 2, 1961, Ketchum, ID

Audrey Hepburn was a British actress, model, dancer and humanitarian. Recognised as a film and fashion icon, Hepburn was active during Hollywood's Golden Age. Wikipedia
Born: May 4, 1929, Ixelles, Belgium
Died: January 20, 1993, Tolochenaz, Switzerland

Oliver Napoleon Hill was an American self-help author. He is known best for his book Think and Grow Rich which is among the 10 best-selling self-help books of all time. Wikipedia
Born: October 26, 1883, Pound, VA
Died: November 8, 1970, South Carolina

John C. McHugh M.D.

Gordon Bitner Hinckley was an American religious leader and author who served as the 15th President of The Church of Jesus Christ of Latter-day Saints from March 12, 1995, until his death. Wikipedia
Born: June 23, 1910, Salt Lake City, UT
Died: January 27, 2008, Salt Lake City, UT

Louis Leo Holtz is a former American football player, coach, and analyst. He served as the head football coach at The College of William & Mary, North Carolina State University, and Notre Dame. Wikipedia
Born: January 6, 1937, Follansbee, WV

Elbert Green Hubbard was an American writer, publisher, artist, and philosopher. Raised in Hudson, Illinois, he had early success as a traveling salesman for the Larkin Soap Company. Wikipedia
Born: June 19, 1856, Bloomington, IL
Died: May 7, 1915, Republic of Ireland

Victor Marie Hugo was a French poet, novelist, and dramatist of the Romantic movement. Hugo is considered to be one of the greatest and best-known French writers. Wikipedia
Born: February 26, 1802, Besançon, France
Died: May 22, 1885, Paris, France

Thomas Henry Huxley was an English biologist specializing in comparative anatomy. He is known as "Darwin's Bulldog" for his advocacy of Charles Darwin's theory of evolution. Wikipedia
Born: May 4, 1825, Ealing, London, United Kingdom
Died: June 29, 1895, Eastbourne, United Kingdom

Aldous Leonard Huxley was an English writer, novelist, philosopher, and prominent member of the Huxley family. He graduated from Balliol College at the University of Oxford with a first class honors in English literature. Wikipedia
Born: July 26, 1894, Godalming, United Kingdom
Died: November 22, 1963, Los Angeles, CA

Lido Anthony "Lee" Iacocca is an American automobile executive best known for spearheading the development of Ford Mustang and Pinto cars, while at the Ford Motor Company in the 1960s.
Born: October 15, 1924, Allentown, PA

Jeffrey Paul "Jeph" Jacques is an American cartoonist who writes and draws the web comics Questionable Content, Alice Grove, and DORD. Wikipedia
Born: June 17, 1980, Rockville, MD

William James was an American philosopher and psychologist who was also trained as a physician. The first educator to offer a psychology course in the United States. Wikipedia
Born: January 11, 1842, New York City, NY
Died: August 26, 1910, Chocorua, NH

Steven Paul Jobs was an American entrepreneur, business magnate, inventor, and industrial designer. He was the chairman, chief executive officer, and co-founder of Apple. Wikipedia
Born: February 24, 1955, San Francisco, CA
Died: October 5, 2011, Palo Alto, CA

Dwayne Douglas Johnson, also known by his ring name The Rock, is an American actor and professional wrestler. He was a college football player for the University of Miami, where he won a national championship on the 1991 Miami Hurricanes team. Wikipedia
Born: May 2, 1972, Hayward, CA

Patrick Spencer Johnson was an American physician and author, known for the Value Tales series of children's books, and for his 1998 motivational book Who Moved My Cheese?, which recurred on the New York ... Wikipedia
Born: November 24, 1938, Watertown, SD
Died: July 3, 2017, San Diego, CA

Samuel Johnson, often referred to as Dr. Johnson, was an English writer who made lasting contributions to English literature as a poet, essayist, moralist, literary critic, biographer, editor and lexicographer. Wikipedia
Born: September 18, 1709, Lichfield, United Kingdom
Died: December 13, 1784, London, United Kingdom

Carl Gustav Jung was a Swiss psychiatrist and psychoanalyst who founded analytical psychology. His work has been influential not only in psychiatry but also in anthropology, archaeology, literature, philosophy, and religious studies. Wikipedia
Born: July 26, 1875, Kesswil, Switzerland
Died: June 6, 1961, Küsnacht, Switzerland

John C. McHugh M.D.

William Aloysius Keane, better known as Bil Keane, was an American cartoonist most notable for his work on the newspaper comic The Family Circus. It began in 1960 and continues in syndication, drawn by his son Jeff Keane. Wikipedia
Born: October 5, 1922, Philadelphia, PA
Died: November 8, 2011, Paradise Valley, AZ

Helen Adams Keller was an American author, political activist, and lecturer. She was the first deaf-blind person to earn a bachelor of arts degree. Wikipedia
Born: June 27, 1880, Tuscumbia, AL
Died: June 1, 1968, Easton, CT

Jacqueline Lee "Jackie" Kennedy Onassis was the wife of the 35th President of the United States, John F. Kennedy, and First Lady of the United States from 1961 until his assassination in 1963. Wikipedia
Born: July 28, 1929, Southampton, NY
Died: May 19, 1994, Manhattan, New York City, NY

Jack Kerouac was an American novelist and poet of French-Canadian descent. He is considered a literary iconoclast and, alongside William S. Burroughs and Allen Ginsberg, a pioneer of the Beat Generation. Wikipedia
Born: March 12, 1922, Lowell
Died: October 21, 1969, St. Anthony's Hospital, St. Petersburg, FL

Riley B. King, known professionally as B.B. King, was an American blues singer, electric guitarist, songwriter, and record producer. Wikipedia
Born: September 16, 1925, Itta Bena, MS
Died: May 14, 2015, Las Vegas, NV

Martin Luther King Jr. was an American Baptist minister and activist who became the most visible spokesperson and leader in the civil rights movement. Wikipedia
Born: January 15, 1929, Atlanta, GA
Assassinated: April 4, 1968, Memphis, TN

Joseph Rudyard Kipling was an English journalist, short-story writer, poet, and novelist. Kipling's works of fiction include The Jungle Book, Kim, and many short stories, including "The Man Who Would Be King". Wikipedia
Born: December 30, 1865, Mumbai, India

Died: January 18, 1936, Middlesex Hospital, London

The 14th Dalai Lama is the current Dalai Lama. Dalai Lamas are important monks of the Gelug school, the newest school of Tibetan Buddhism which is formally headed by the Ganden Tripas. Wikipedia
Born: July 6, 1935, Taktser

Anne Lamott is an American novelist and non-fiction writer. She is also a progressive political activist, public speaker, and writing teacher. Based in the San Francisco Bay Area, her nonfiction works are largely autobiographical. Wikipedia
Born: April 10, 1954, San Francisco, CA

Thomas Charles Lasorda is a former Major League Baseball pitcher who is best known for his two decades as manager of the Los Angeles Dodgers. Wikipedia
Born: September 22, 1927, Norristown, PA

Laozi, was an ancient Chinese philosopher and writer. He is known as the reputed author of the Tao Te Ching, the founder of philosophical Taoism, and a deity in religious Taoism and traditional Chinese religions. Wikipedia
Born: 604 BC, Henan, China
Died: 531 BC, China

Lee Jun-fan, known professionally as Bruce Lee, was a Hong Kong and American actor, film director, martial artist, martial arts instructor, philosopher and founder of the martial arts. Wikipedia
Born: November 27, 1940, San Francisco Chinese Hospital, San Francisco, CA
Died: July 20, 1973, Kowloon Tong, Hong Kong

Nelle Harper Lee, better known by her pen name Harper Lee, was an American novelist widely known for To Kill a Mockingbird, published in 1960. Wikipedia
Born: April 28, 1926, Monroeville, AL
Died: February 19, 2016, Monroeville, AL

Clive Staples Lewis was a British novelist, poet, academic, medievalist, literary critic, essayist, lay theologian, broadcaster, lecturer, and Christian apologist. He held academic positions at both Oxford University and Cambridge University. Wikipedia
Born: November 29, 1898, Belfast

John C. McHugh M.D.

Died: November 22, 1963, Oxford, United Kingdom

Christoph Lichtenberg was a German physicist, satirist, and Anglophile. As a scientist, he was the first to hold a professorship explicitly dedicated to experimental physics in Germany. Wikipedia
Born: July 1, 1742, Ober-Ramstadt, Germany
Died: February 24, 1799, Göttingen, Germany

Joshua Loth Liebman was an American rabbi and best-selling author, best known for the book Peace of Mind, which spent more than a year at #1 on the New York Times Best Seller list. Wikipedia
Born: 1907, Hamilton, OH
Died: 1948, Boston, MA

Abraham Lincoln was an American statesman and lawyer who served as the 16th President of the United States from March 1861 until his assassination in April 1865. Wikipedia
Born: February 12, 1809, Hodgenville, KY
Assassinated: April 15, 1865, Petersen House, Washington, D.C.

Arthur Gordon "Art" Linkletter was a Canadian-born American radio and television personality. He was the host of House Party, which ran on CBS radio and television for 25 years, and People Are Funny, on NBC radio and TV for 19 years. Wikipedia
Born: July 17, 1912, Moose Jaw, Canada
Died: May 26, 2010, Los Angeles, CA

John Locke was an English philosopher and physician, widely regarded as one of the most influential of Enlightenment thinkers and commonly known as the "Father of Liberalism". Wikipedia
Born: August 29, 1632, Wrington, United Kingdom
Died: October 28, 1704, High Laver, United Kingdom

Vincent Thomas Lombardi was an American football player, coach, and executive in the National Football League. Wikipedia
Born: June 11, 1913, Brooklyn, New York City, NY
Died: September 3, 1970, Washington, D.C.

Henry Wadsworth Longfellow was an American poet and educator whose works include "Paul Revere's Ride", The Song of Hiawatha, and Evangeline. Wikipedia
Born: February 27, 1807, Portland, ME
Died: March 24, 1882, Cambridge, MA

James Russell Lowell was an American Romantic poet, critic, editor, and diplomat. He is associated with the Fireside Poets, a group of New England writers who were among the first American poets that rivaled the popularity of British poets. Wikipedia
Born: February 22, 1819, Cambridge
Died: August 12, 1891, Cambridge

Douglas MacArthur was an American five-star general and Field Marshal of the Philippine Army. He was Chief of Staff of the United States Army during the 1930s and played a prominent role in the Pacific theater during World War II. Wikipedia
Born: January 26, 1880, Little Rock, AR
Died: April 5, 1964, Walter Reed National Military Medical Center

Niccolò di Bernardo dei Machiavelli was an Italian diplomat, politician, historian, philosopher, humanist, and writer of the Renaissance period. He has often been called the father of modern political science. Wikipedia
Born: May 3, 1469, Florence, Italy
Died: June 21, 1527, Florence, Italy

Harvey Mackay is a businessman, author and syndicated columnist with Universal Uclick. His weekly column gives career and inspirational advice and is featured in over 100 newspapers. Wikipedia
Born: 1932, Saint Paul, MN

Maxwell Maltz was an American cosmetic surgeon and author of Psycho-Cybernetics, which was a system of ideas that he claimed could improve one's self-image. In turn, the person would lead a more successful and fulfilling life. Wikipedia
Born: March 10, 1889, New York City, NY
Died: April 7, 1975

Nelson Rolihlahla Mandela was a South African anti-apartheid revolutionary, political leader, and philanthropist, who served as President of South Africa from 1994 to 1999. Wikipedia
Born: July 18, 1918, Mvezo, South Africa
Died: December 5, 2013, Houghton Estate, City of Johannesburg Metropolitan Municipality, South Africa

Horace Mann was an American educational reformer and Whig politician dedicated to promoting public education. He served in the Massachusetts State legislature. Wikipedia

John C. McHugh M.D.

Born: May 4, 1796, Franklin, MA
Died: August 2, 1859, Yellow Springs, OH

Paul Thomas Mann was a German novelist, short story writer, social critic, philanthropist, essayist, and the 1929 Nobel Prize in Literature laureate. Wikipedia
Born: June 6, 1875, Free City of Lübeck
Died: August 12, 1955, Zürich, Switzerland

Mickey Charles Mantle, nicknamed The Commerce Comet and The Mick, was an American professional baseball player. Wikipedia
Born: October 20, 1931, Spavinaw, OK
Died: August 13, 1995, Baylor University Medical Center, Dallas, TX

Rocco Francis Marchegiano, best known as Rocky Marciano, was an American professional boxer who competed from 1947 to 1955, and held the world heavyweight title from 1952 to 1956. Wikipedia
Born: September 1, 1923, Brockton
Died: August 31, 1969, Newton, IA

Edwin Markham was an American poet. From 1923 to 1931 he was Poet Laureate of Oregon. Wikipedia
Born: April 23, 1852, Oregon City, OR
Died: March 7, 1940, Staten Island, New York City, NY

James Norman Mattis is a retired United States Marine Corps general who is the 26th and current United States Secretary of Defense, serving in the Cabinet of Donald Trump. Wikipedia
Born: September 8, 1950, Pullman, WA

John Calvin Maxwell is an American author, speaker, and pastor who has written many books, primarily focusing on leadership. Titles include The 21 Irrefutable Laws of Leadership and The 21 Indispensable Qualities of a Leader. Wikipedia
Born: February 20, 1947, Garden City, MI

David Gaub McCullough is an American author, narrator, historian, and lecturer. He is a two-time winner of the Pulitzer Prize and the National Book Award and a recipient of the Presidential Medal of ... Wikipedia
Born: July 7, 1933, Pittsburgh

Herman Melville was an American novelist, short story writer, and poet of the American Renaissance period. His best known works

204

include Typee, a romantic account of his experiences in Polynesian life, and his whaling novel Moby-Dick. Wikipedia
Born: August 1, 1819, Manhattan, New York City, NY
Died: September 28, 1891, New York City, NY

Henry Louis Mencken was an American journalist, satirist, cultural critic and scholar of American English. Wikipedia
Born: September 12, 1880, Baltimore, MD
Died: January 29, 1956, Baltimore, MD

John Stuart Mill was a British philosopher, political economist and civil servant. One of the most influential thinkers in the history of liberalism, he contributed widely to social theory, political theory and political economy. Wikipedia
Born: May 20, 1806, Pentonville, London, United Kingdom
Died: May 8, 1873, Avignon, France

Daniel Jay Millman is an American author and lecturer in the personal development field. Wikipedia
Born: February 22, 1946, Los Angeles, CA

Marilyn Monroe was an American actress, model and singer. Famous for playing comic 'blonde bombshell' characters, she became one of the most popular sex symbols of the 1950s and was emblematic of the era's attitudes towards sexuality. Wikipedia
Born: June 1, 1926, Los Angeles, CA
Died: August 5, 1962, Brentwood, Los Angeles, CA

Juan María Montalvo Fiallos was an Ecuadorian author and essayist. Wikipedia
Born: April 13, 1832, Ambato, Ecuador
Died: January 17, 1889, Paris, France

John Pierpont Morgan Sr. was an American financier and banker who dominated corporate finance and industrial consolidation in the United States of America in the late 19th and early 20th centuries. Wikipedia
Born: April 17, 1837, Hartford, CT
Died: March 31, 1913, Rome, Italy

Audie Leon Murphy was one of the most decorated American combat soldiers of World War II, receiving every military combat award for valor available from the U.S. Army, as well as French and Belgian awards for heroism. Wikipedia

John C. McHugh M.D.

Born: June 20, 1925, Kingston, TX
Died: May 28, 1971, Catawba, VA

Sir Isaac Newton was an English mathematician, astronomer,
theologian and physicist who is widely recognised as one of the
most influential scientists of all time and a key figure in the
scientific revolution. Wikipedia
Born: December 25, 1642, Woolsthorpe Manor, United Kingdom
Died: March 31, 1727, Kensington, London, United Kingdom

Karl Paul Reinhold Niebuhr was an American theologian, ethicist,
commentator on politics and public affairs, and professor at Union
Theological Seminary for more than 30 years. Wikipedia
Born: June 21, 1892, Wright City, MO
Died: June 1, 1971, Stockbridge, MA

Friedrich Wilhelm Nietzsche was a German philosopher, cultural
critic, composer, poet, philologist, and Latin and Greek scholar
whose work has exerted a profound influence on Western
philosophy and modern intellectual history. Wikipedia
Born: October 15, 1844, Röcken, Germany
Died: August 25, 1900, Weimar, Germany

 Inazō Nitobe was a Japanese agricultural economist, author,
educator, diplomat, politician, and Christian during the pre-World
War II period. Wikipedia
Born: September 1, 1862, Morioka, Iwate Prefecture, Japan
Died: October 15, 1933, Victoria, Canada

Charles "Chuck" Carmin Noble was an American Major General
and engineer who worked on the Manhattan Project, led
construction in Nuremberg after World War II, developed the
early American ICBM program. Wikipedia
Died: August 16, 2003

Pierre Morad Omidyar is an entrepreneur and philanthropist. He is
the founder of the eBay auction site where he served as chairman
from 1998 to 2015. He became a billionaire at the age of 31 with
eBay's 1998 initial public offering. Wikipedia
Born: June 21, 1967, Paris, France

Sir William Osler, 1st Baronet, was a Canadian physician and one
of the four founding professors of Johns Hopkins
Hospital. Wikipedia
Born: July 12, 1849, Bradford West Gwillimbury, Canada
Died: December 29, 1919, Oxford, United Kingdom

Leroy Robert "Satchel" Paige was an American Negro league
baseball and Major League Baseball pitcher who became a legend
in his own lifetime by being known as perhaps the best pitcher in
baseball history. Wikipedia
Born: July 7, 1906, Mobile, AL
Died: June 8, 1982, Kansas City, MO

Theodore Parker was an American Transcendentalist and
reforming minister of the Unitarian church. A reformer and
abolitionist, his words and popular quotations would later inspire
speeches by Abraham Lincoln and Martin Luther King,
Jr. Wikipedia
Born: August 24, 1810, Lexington, MA
Died: May 10, 1860, Florence, Italy

Rosa Louise McCauley Parks was an activist in the Civil Rights
Movement, whom the United States Congress called "the first lady
of civil rights" and "the mother of the freedom
movement". Wikipedia
Born: February 4, 1913, Tuskegee, AL
Died: October 24, 2005, Detroit, MI

Louis Pasteur was a French biologist, microbiologist and chemist
renowned for his discoveries of the principles of vaccination,
microbial fermentation and pasteurization. Wikipedia
Born: December 27, 1822, Dole, France
Died: September 28, 1895, Marnes-la-Coquette, France

Maharishi Patanjali is a saint who is believed to have lived some
time during the 2nd century BCE. Known for his treatise on Yoga,
entitled "Patanjali Yoga Sutra."

General George Smith Patton Jr. was a senior officer of the United
States Army who commanded the U.S. Seventh Army in the
Mediterranean and European theaters of World War II, but is best
known for his leadership of the U.S. Wikipedia
Born: November 11, 1885, San Gabriel, CA
Died: December 21, 1945, Heidelberg, Germany

John C. McHugh M.D.

Norman Vincent Peale was an American minister and author known for his work in popularizing the concept of positive thinking, especially through his best-selling book The Power of Positive Thinking. Wikipedia
Born: May 31, 1898, Bowersville, OH
Died: December 24, 1993, Pawling, NY

William Penn was the son of Sir William Penn, and was an English real estate entrepreneur, philosopher, early Quaker, and founder of the State of Pennsylvania, the English North American colony and the future Commonwealth of Pennsylvania. Wikipedia
Born: October 14, 1644, London, United Kingdom
Died: July 30, 1718, Ruscombe, United Kingdom

Austin Phelps was an American Congregational minister and educator. He was for 10 years President of the Andover Theological Seminary and his writings became standard textbooks for Christian theological education and remain in print today. Wikipedia
Born: January 7, 1820, West Brookfield, MA
Died: October 13, 1890, Bar Harbor, ME

Oail Andrew "Bum" Phillips was an American football coach at the high school, college and professional levels. Wikipedia
Born: September 29, 1923, Orange, TX
Died: October 18, 2013, Goliad, TX

Pablo Picasso was a Spanish painter, sculptor, printmaker, ceramicist, stage designer, poet and playwright who spent most of his adult life in France. Wikipedia
Born: October 25, 1881, Málaga, Spain
Died: April 8, 1973, Mougins, France

Plato was a philosopher in Classical Greece and the founder of the Academy in Athens, the first institution of higher learning in the Western world. Wikipedia
Born: Classical Athens-Died: Classical Athens

Pope John XXIII was head of the Catholic Church and ruler of the Vatican City State from 28 October 1958 to his death in 1963 and was canonized on 27 April 2014.
Born: November 25, 1881, Sotto il Monte Giovanni XXIII, Italy
Died: June 3, 1963, Apostolic Palace, Vatican City

Ezra Weston Loomis Pound was an expatriate American poet and critic, as well as a major figure in the early modernist movement. Wikipedia
Born: October 30, 1885, Hailey, ID
Died: November 1, 1972, Venice, Italy

Colin Luther Powell is an American elder statesman and a retired four-star general in the United States Army. Powell was born in Harlem as the son of Jamaican immigrants. Wikipedia
Born: April 5, 1937, Harlem, New York City, NY

Ayn Rand was a Russian-American novelist, philosopher, playwright, and screenwriter. She is known for her two best-selling novels, The Fountainhead and Atlas Shrugged, and for developing a philosophical system she called Objectivism. Wikipedia
Born: February 2, 1905, Saint Petersburg, Russia
Died: March 6, 1982, Manhattan, New York City, NY

Donald Thomas "Don" Regan was the 66th United States Secretary of the Treasury from 1981 to 1985 and the White House Chief of Staff from 1985 to 1987 in the Ronald Reagan Administration. Wikipedia
Born: December 21, 1918, Cambridge, MA
Died: June 10, 2003, Williamsburg, VA

Lucas Remmerswall is the author of A-Z of 13 Habits: Inspired by Warren Buffett.

Tony Robbins, born Anthony J. Mahavoric, is an American author, entrepreneur, philanthropist and life coach. Robbins is known for his infomercials, seminars, and self-help books including Unlimited Power and Awaken the Giant Within. Wikipedia
Born: February 29, 1960, North Hollywood, CA

John Davison Rockefeller Sr. was an American oil industry business magnate, industrialist, and philanthropist. He is widely considered the wealthiest American of all time, and the richest person in modern history. Wikipedia
Born: July 8, 1839, Richford, NY
Died: May 23, 1937, Ormond Beach, FL

John C. McHugh M.D.

Knute Kenneth Rockne was a Norwegian-American football player and coach at the University of Notre Dame. Rockne is regarded as one of the greatest coaches in college football history. Wikipedia
Born: March 4, 1888, Voss, Norway
Died: March 31, 1931, Bazaar, KS

Carl Ransom Rogers was an American psychologist and among the founders of the humanistic approach to psychology. Wikipedia
Born: January 8, 1902, Oak Park, IL
Died: February 4, 1987, San Diego, CA

Emanuel James "Jim" Rohn was an American entrepreneur, author and motivational speaker. Wikipedia
Born: September 17, 1930, Yakima, WA
Died: December 5, 2009, West Hills, Los Angeles, CA

Richard Rohr is an American Franciscan friar ordained to the priesthood in the Roman Catholic Church in 1970. Wikipedia
Born: March 20, 1943, Topeka, KS

Anna Eleanor Roosevelt was an American politician, diplomat and activist. She was the longest-serving First Lady of the United States, having held the post from March 1933 to April 1945 during her ...Wikipedia
Born: October 11, 1884, New York City, NY
Died: November 7, 1962, 74th Street, New York City, NY
Spouse: Franklin D. Roosevelt (m. 1905–1945)

Theodore Roosevelt Jr. was an American statesman, author, explorer, soldier, and naturalist, who served as the 26th President of the United States from 1901 to 1909. Wikipedia
Born: October 27, 1858, Manhattan, New York City, NY
Died: January 6, 1919, Sagamore Hill, Town of Oyster Bay, NY
Presidential term: September 14, 1901 – March 4, 1909

Joanne Rowling, who writes under the pen names J. K. Rowling and Robert Galbraith, is a British novelist and screenwriter who is best known for writing the Harry Potter fantasy series. Wikipedia
Born: July 31, 1965, Yate, United Kingdom

Howard Joseph Ruff was a financial adviser and writer of the pro-hard money investing newsletter The Ruff Times. Wikipedia
Born: 1931, Berkeley, CA
Died: November 12, 2016, Lehi, UT

George Herman "Babe" Ruth Jr. was an American professional baseball player whose career in Major League Baseball spanned 22 seasons, from 1914 through 1935. Wikipedia
Born: February 6, 1895, Pigtown, Baltimore, MD
Died: August 16, 1948, Manhattan, New York City, NY

Antoine de Saint-Exupéry was a French writer, poet, aristocrat, journalist, and pioneering aviator. He became a laureate of several of France's highest literary awards and also won the U.S. National Book Award. Wikipedia
Born: June 29, 1900, Lyon, France
Died: July 31, 1944, Marseille, France

Carl August Sandburg was a Swedish-American poet, writer, and editor. He won three Pulitzer Prizes: two for his poetry and one for his biography of Abraham Lincoln. Wikipedia
Born: January 6, 1878, Galesburg, IL
Died: July 22, 1967, Flat Rock, Mount Airy Township, NC

Jorge Agustín Nicolás Ruiz de Santayana Borrás, known in English as George Santayana, was a philosopher, essayist, poet, and novelist. Wikipedia
Born: December 16, 1863, Madrid, Spain
Died: September 26, 1952, Rome, Italy

Jean-Paul Charles Aymard Sartre was a French philosopher, playwright, novelist, political activist, biographer, and literary critic. Wikipedia
Born: June 21, 1905, Paris, France

Marilyn vos Savant is an American who is known for having the highest recorded IQ according to the Guinness Book of Records, a competitive category the publication has since retired. Savant is a magazine columnist, author, lecturer, and playwright. Wikipedia
Born: August 11, 1946, St. Louis, MO

Charles Monroe Schulz, nicknamed Sparky, was an American cartoonist best known for the comic strip Peanuts. Wikipedia
Born: November 26, 1922, Minneapolis, MN
Died: February 12, 2000, Santa Rosa, CA
Books: Happiness is ... a warm puppy, Peanuts Every Sunday

Charles Michael Schwab was an American steel magnate. Under his leadership, Bethlehem Steel became the second largest steel maker in the United States, and one of the most important heavy manufacturers in the world. Wikipedia
Born: February 18, 1862, Williamsburg, PA
Died: September 18, 1939, New York

Albert Schweitzer was a French-German theologian, organist, writer, humanitarian, philosopher, and physician. Wikipedia
Born: January 14, 1875, Kaysersberg, France
Died: September 4, 1965, Lambaréné, Gabon

Seal (Henry Olusegun Adeola Samuel) is a British singer and songwriter. He has sold more than 20 million records worldwide and is known for his international hits. Wikipedia
Born: February 19, 1963, Paddington, London, United Kingdom

Seneca the Younger, fully Lucius Annaeus Seneca and also known simply as Seneca, was a Roman Stoic philosopher, statesman, dramatist, and in one work humorist of the Silver Age of Latin literature. Wikipedia
Born: 4 BC, Córdoba, Spain
Died: 65 AD, Rome, Italy

Theodor Seuss "Ted" Geisel was a German-American author, political cartoonist, poet, animator, book publisher, and artist, best known for authoring more than 60 children's books under the pen name Doctor Seuss. Wikipedia
Born: March 2, 1904, Springfield, MA
Died: September 24, 1991, La Jolla, CA

William Shakespeare was an English poet, playwright and actor, widely regarded as the greatest writer in the English language and the world's pre-eminent dramatist. He is often called England's national poet and the "Bard of Avon". Wikipedia
Born: 1564, Stratford-upon-Avon, United Kingdom
Died: April 23, 1616, Stratford-upon-Avon, United Kingdom

George Bernard Shaw, known at his insistence simply as Bernard Shaw, was an Irish playwright, critic, polemicist, and political activist who held both Irish and British citizenship. Wikipedia
Born: July 26, 1856, Portobello, Dublin, Republic of Ireland
Died: November 2, 1950, Ayot St Lawrence, United Kingdom

Samuel Shem is the pen-name of the American psychiatrist
Stephen Joseph Bergman. His main works are The House of God
and Mount Misery, both fictional but close-to-real first-hand
descriptions of the training of doctors in the United
States. Wikipedia
Born: 1944, Hudson, NY

Samuel Smiles, was a Scottish author and government reformer
who campaigned on a Chartist platform. But he concluded that
more progress would come from new attitudes than from new
laws. Wikipedia
Born: December 23, 1812, Haddington, United Kingdom
Died: April 16, 1904, Kensington, London, United Kingdom

Socrates was a classical Greek philosopher credited as one of the
founders of Western philosophy, and as being the first moral
philosopher, of the western ethical tradition of thought. Wikipedia
Born: Alopece
Died: 399 BC, Classical Athens

Sophocles is one of three ancient Greek tragedians whose plays
have survived. His first plays were written later than those of
Aeschylus, and earlier than or contemporary with those of
Euripides. Wikipedia
Born: Hippeios Colonus, Athens, Greece
Died: 406 BC, Classical Athens

Brent Jay Spiner is an American actor, comedian, and singer best
known for his portrayal of the android Lieutenant Commander
Data in the television series Star Trek: The Next Generation and
four subsequent films. Wikipedia
Born: February 2, 1949, Houston, TX

Harriet Elisabeth Beecher Stowe was an American abolitionist and
author. She came from the Beecher family, a famous religious
family, and is best known for her novel Uncle Tom's Cabin, which
depicts ... Wikipedia
Born: June 14, 1811, Litchfield, CT
Died: July 1, 1896, Hartford, CT

Publilius Syrus, was a Latin writer, best known for his sententiae.
He was a Syrian who was brought as a slave to Italy, but by his wit
and talent he won the favour of his master, who freed and educated
him. Wikipedia

John C. McHugh M.D.

Born: 85 BC

Nikola Tesla was a Serbian-American inventor, electrical engineer, mechanical engineer, physicist, and futurist who is best known for his contributions to the design of the modern alternating current electricity supply system. Wikipedia
Born: July 10, 1856, Smiljan, Croatia
Died: January 7, 1943, Wyndham New Yorker Hotel, New York City, NY

Clarence Thomas is an American judge, lawyer, and government official who currently serves as an Associate Justice of the Supreme Court of the United States. Wikipedia
Born: June 23, 1948, Pin Point, GA

Helen Amelia Thomas was an American reporter and author best known for her longtime membership in the White House press corps. Wikipedia
Born: August 4, 1920, Winchester, KY
Died: July 20, 2013, Washington, D.C.

Henry David Thoreau was an American essayist, poet, philosopher, abolitionist, naturalist, tax resister, development critic, surveyor, and historian. Wikipedia
Born: July 12, 1817, Concord
Died: May 6, 1862, Concord

Alexis Charles Henri Clérel, Viscount de Tocqueville was a French diplomat, political scientist, and historian. He was best known for his works Democracy in America and The Old Regime and the Revolution. Wikipedia
Born: July 29, 1805, Paris, France
Died: April 16, 1859, Cannes, France

Arnold Joseph Toynbee was a British historian, philosopher of history, research professor of international history at the London School of Economics and the University of London and author of numerous books. Wikipedia
Born: April 14, 1889, London, United Kingdom
Died: October 22, 1975, York, United Kingdom

Harry S. Truman was an American statesman who served as the 33rd President of the United States, taking the office upon the death of Franklin D. Roosevelt. Wikipedia

Born: May 8, 1884, Lamar, MO
Died: December 26, 1972, Kansas City, MO

Harriet Tubman was an American abolitionist, humanitarian, and an armed scout and spy for the United States Army during the American Civil War. Wikipedia
Born: 1822, Dorchester County, MD
Died: March 10, 1913, Auburn, NY

Mark Twain (Samuel Langhorne Clemens) was an American writer, humorist, entrepreneur, publisher, and lecturer. Wikipedia
Born: November 30, 1835, Florida, MO
Died: April 21, 1910, Redding, CT

Aisha N. Tyler is an American talk show host, actress, author, producer, writer, and director. She is known for portraying Andrea Marino in the first season of Ghost Whisperer. Wikipedia
Born: September 18, 1970, San Francisco, CA

Sun Tzu was a Chinese general, military strategist, and philosopher who lived in the Eastern Zhou period of ancient China. Wikipedia
Born: 544 BC, Qi-Died: 496 BC, Wu

Voltaire (François-Marie Arouet) was a French Enlightenment writer, historian and philosopher famous for his wit, his attacks on the established Catholic Church and Christianity. Wikipedia
Born: November 21, 1694, Paris, France
Died: May 30, 1778, Paris, France

Richard Duane "Rick" Warren is an American evangelical Christian pastor and author. He is the founder and senior pastor of Saddleback Church, an evangelical megachurch in Lake Forest, California. Wikipedia
Born: January 28, 1954, San Jose, CA

John Wayne (Marion Mitchell Morrison) known professionally as John Wayne and nicknamed Duke, was an American actor and filmmaker. An Academy Award-winner for True Grit, Wayne was among the top box office draws for three decades. Wikipedia
Born: May 26, 1907, Winterset, IA
Died: June 11, 1979, Los Angeles, CA

John Francis "Jack" Welch Jr. is an American retired business executive, author, and chemical engineer. He was chairman and CEO of General Electric between 1981 and 2001.
Born: November 19, 1935, Peabody, MA

Mary Jane "Mae" West was an American actress, singer, playwright, screenwriter, comedian, and sex symbol.
Born: August 17, 1893, Bushwick, New York City, NY
Died: November 22, 1980, Hollywood, Los Angeles, CA

John Greenleaf Whittier was an American Quaker poet and advocate of the abolition of slavery in the United States.
Born: December 17, 1807, Haverhill, MA
Died: September 7, 1892, Hampton Falls, NH

Eliezer "Elie" Wiesel was a Romanian-born American Jewish writer, professor, Nobel Laureate, and Holocaust survivor.
Born: September 30, 1928, Sighetu Marmației, Romania
Died: July 2, 2016, Upper East Side, New York City, NY

Oscar Wilde was an Irish poet and playwright. After writing in different forms throughout the 1880s, he became one of London's most popular playwrights.
Born: October 16, 1854, Westland Row, Dublin, Ireland
Died: November 30, 1900, French Third Republic

Thomas Woodrow Wilson was an American statesman and academic who served as the 28th President of the United States.
Born: December 28, 1856, Staunton, Virginia, VA
Died: February 3, 1924, Washington, D.C.

Winnie the Pooh is a fictional character and the title character from the Disney media franchise based on A. A. Milne's Winnie-the-Pooh. Home: Hundred Acre Wood

John Robert Wooden was an American basketball player and head coach at the University of California at Los Angeles. Wikipedia
Born: October 14, 1910, Hall, IN
Died: June 4, 2010, Los Angeles, CA

Harry Hinton "Zig" Ziglar was an American salesman, author and motivational speaker. Born: November 6, 1926, AL
Died: 2012, Plano, TX

"Wasting his and others study hall time; laughing, talking, etc."

"Talkative, disturbs class and me by actions."

"Disturbs others; sulks when corrected. A good kid but he hasn't learned to think of others enough!"

My conduct report card from 9th grade-You see we all start out as weeds but...we don't have to stay one!

Carpe diem!

John C. McHugh M.D.

Kipling's *If*-The First Self-Help Poem

My mother's favorite adage from her favorite poem-Fill the unforgiving minute with sixty seconds' worth of distance run!

If you can keep your head when all about you
Are losing theirs and blaming it on you,
If you can trust yourself when all men doubt you,
But make allowance for their doubting too;
If you can wait and not be tired by waiting,
Or being lied about, don't deal in lies,
Or being hated, don't give way to hating,
And yet don't look too good, nor talk too wise:

If you can dream-and not make dreams your master;
If you can think-and not make thoughts your aim;
If you can meet with Triumph and Disaster
And treat those two impostors just the same;
If you can bear to hear the truth you've spoken
Twisted by knaves to make a trap for fools,
Or watch the things you gave your life to, broken,
And stoop and build 'em up with worn-out tools:

If you can make one heap of all your winnings
And risk it on one turn of pitch-and-toss,
And lose, and start again at your beginnings
And never breathe a word about your loss;
If you can force your heart and nerve and sinew
To serve your turn long after they are gone,
And so hold on when there is nothing in you
Except the Will which says to them: 'Hold on!'

If you can talk with crowds and keep your virtue,
Or walk with Kings-nor lose the common touch,
If neither foes nor loving friends can hurt you,
If all men count with you, but none too much;
If you can fill the unforgiving minute
With sixty seconds' worth of distance run,
Yours is the Earth and everything that's in it,
And-which is more you'll be a Man, my son!

And Finally...

Be Grateful

Gratitude is not only the greatest of virtues,
but the parent of all the others.
-Marcus Tullius Cicero

Be Generous

What I spent, is gone; what I kept, I lost; but
what I gave away will be mine forever.
-Ethel Percy Andrus

Be Kind

Be kind whenever possible. It is always
possible.
-Dalai Lama

My brothers and I on the steps of our grandmother's house
at 103 N. Lewis St. around the time we moved in with her,
circa 1968.